BIKING BEIJING

Diana B. Kingsbury

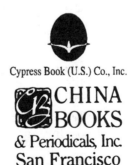

Cypress Book (U.S.) Co., Inc.

CHINA BOOKS
& Periodicals, Inc.
San Francisco

Photos by: Zhou Youma
　　　　　 Diana B. Kingsbury

Maps by: Zhang Guofu
Designed by: Linda Revel
Edited by: Foster Stockwell and Lisa Ryan

Copyright © 1994 by Diana B. Kingsbury. All rights reserved.

No part of this book may be used or reproduced in any manner whatsoever without permission in writing from the publisher. Address inquiries to China Books, 2929 24th Street, San Francisco, CA 94110

Library of Congress Catalog Card Number: 94-070303
ISBN 0-8351-2527-0

Printed in the United States of America by:
China Books & Periodicals, Inc. and Cypress Book Company

To Grandma Umland
and Auntie Ruth Austin,
who made the journey possible.

Acknowledgments

This book has been created through the efforts of friends on both sides of the ocean. Thanks go to my editors and colleagues in Beijing: Chen Xiuzheng, Yang Aiwen, Shou Guowei, Yan Xinqiang, and Ren Lingjuan; also to my publishers in San Francisco, Zhang Shaojiang of Cypress Books and Chris Noyes of China Books & Periodicals. To editors Foster Stockwell and Lisa Ryan of China Books for their patience and perseverance. To friends Mary Wiseman and Julie Crawford, for their encouragement over innumerable plates of Xinjiang noodles. To Nick Driver, for his ready supply of information. To those who accompanied me on the bike trips, especially the Camels, for the inspiration and good times. Thanks finally to my parents, who have always been there, no matter how far away I go.

Contents

Introduction 1
Background 7

Setting Off

AUTUMN: The East-West Meridian 11
WINTER: The Northern Lakes Area 49
SPRING: The Old Chinese City 82
SUMMER: Imperial Parklands 113

Slowing Down

What to See 144
What to Do 160
Where to Eat 164
Where to Stay 174

The Mechanics

Traveler Basics 180
Bicycle Rental and Tours 194
Survival Chinese 200
Glossary 204
Index 208

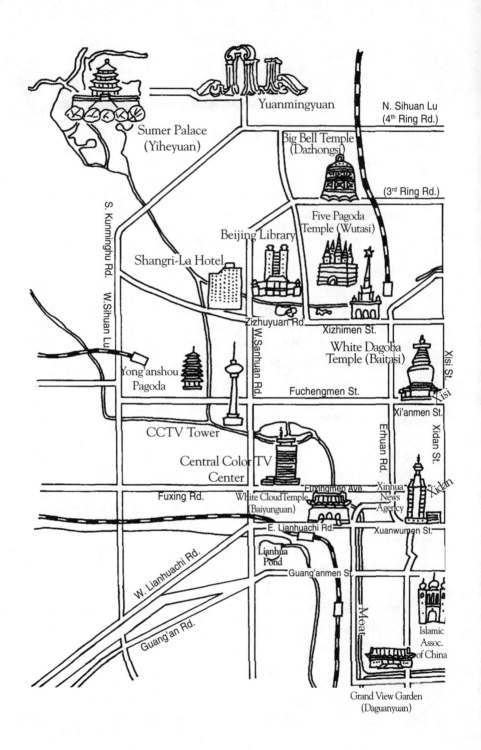

MAP OF

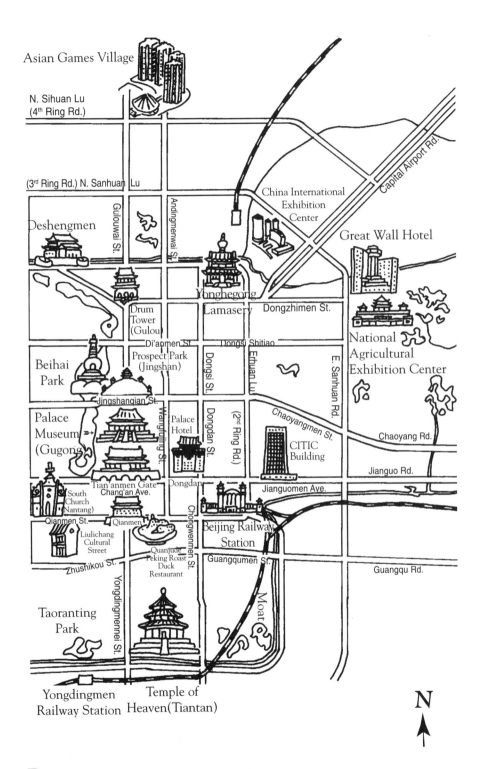

BEIJING

Introduction

At the mention of Beijing, doesn't everyone think of bicycles? There are, after all, eight million of them in the capital alone. News photos invariably portray the masses at rush hour flowing along in their usual river-like way. Popular footage shows bikes streaming down Chang'an Avenue past Tianan'men Square and beyond.

Clichés aside, the standard, heavy-duty two-wheeler remains, for the general public in China, the most common and reliable mode of transportation since the donkey-cart. If you've ever tried to squeeze into a public bus groaning under its load of packed, sweating bodies, you know why. If you've sat fidgeting in a cab while bicycles race past the line of trapped traffic, you know why. If you've explored the back *hutongs* (alleys) of old Beijing, stopping at your leisure to take pictures or chat with the locals, you know why a bicycle is the best investment you'll ever make in this biking capital.

Biking Beijing is an active guide book. It takes you down broad tree-lined avenues where black limos cruise and colorful banners flutter. It takes you through crumbling gray alleyways where gold-toothed grandmas chase after wide-eyed toddlers, and along quiet country roads where the blue sky opens like an umbrella over ripening earth. It takes you to the great landmarks and cultural repositories the Chinese capital is known for, to secluded shops and hidden hutongs few tourists can find. As a guide book, it both leads and describes.

Rent a bike, follow the maps, and you have a self-guided tour. Sit back in your armchair with a cup of tea, and you can comfortably take in the sights, sounds and smells of modern Beijing.

Each takes you to different parts of the city in a different season, running through a full itinerary of sights in one day.

Autumn plunges into the heart of the capital, shooting a straight line from west to east along Chang'an Avenue, then turning back to the busy Wangfujing strip. *Winter* loops around the top of the Second Ring Road (*Erhuan Lu*) before dropping down to visit temples and towers in the Northern Lakes area. *Spring* visits the old "Chinese City" south of the Inner City district, exploring hutongs, ancient markets, and the Temple of Heaven. *Summer* runs northward into the countryside, surveys the old imperial parklands, and passes through the western university district.

The section *What to See* provides further information on sites not covered in the bike trips. *What to Do* covers entertainment options and shopping areas. Restaurants and hotels are described in *Where to Eat* and *Where to Stay*. Details on visas, money, what to bring, health, transportation, bike rental, and survival Chinese are included at the end of the book.

With a city that's changing as quickly as Beijing, a guide book of this sort is out-dated even before it hits the shelves. Prices will have certainly gone up and buildings will have been torn down. The frame of reference that was caught in these words will have passed. If you are planning a trip to China, the newspaper and periodicals will be your best source of information on the economic, social, and political fronts.

Getting Around

For the non-Chinese speaker, biking around Beijing may prove an adventure in sign language and cross-cultural misunderstanding. Some of the locals know enough English to give directions or at least point you on your way. Identifying these scholars among the capital's twelve million people is another matter. Then there are those who have no idea what you're talking about but will helpfully indicate whichever way they think a foreigner on a bicycle is most likely to want to go.

Fortunately, city planners foresaw the day when visiting bicyclists would stand helplessly on street corners scratching their heads in bewilderment. They drew a square in the desert, oriented perfectly to the south, and laid down all major roads to the compass points. They called the square the Forbidden City. For centuries the emperor sat precisely in the center of the square, the city, the country, the universe, facing the sun—the origin of life—in the south.

Modern development has maintained the perfect graph and added several traffic loops around the original square. The Inner City Belt Road is intersected by the well-traveled Second Ring Road, which follows the circle of the former city wall. It is embraced by the concentric Third and Fourth Ring Roads, four-lane speedways dominated by rumbling cargo trucks and clopping horse carts. Aside from the sweeping ring road corners, few curves can be found in Beijing. Even the tangle of hutongs, squared in by the boulevards, though deceptively maze-like, seldom break the straight line rule.

It is difficult to get hopelessly lost in a square city—as long as you know the direction you are headed. Compass points are fixed so permanently in the mind of Beijing residents, they will tell you to turn east or west rather than left or right, even inside a building. Keeping track of the sun's route across the sky is one way to orient yourself. Another is to pin your eye on a prominent high-rise along the city's skyline.

Invest in a good map of the city. An English version is available at the train station, or in any one of the big hotels or major bookstores. Place names, such as the Summer Palace or Workers' Stadium, are usually translated for meaning rather than romanized according to pronunciation of the Chinese characters. You might ask someone to scrawl in the Chinese names of your various destinations beside the English words in preparation for your biking adventure.

Street names, on the other hand, are generally listed in Chinese. You merely match the street signs to names on the map. One problem you will encounter is that streets in Beijing sometimes change names along what appears to be the same stretch of road. Chang'an Avenue, for example, is Fuxingmen Avenue to the west and Jianguomen Avenue to the east. As a further complication, names change according to the road's position inside (*nei*) or outside (*wai*) the former city gates. Jianguomennei Dajie means the avenue (*dajie*) to the inside (*nei*) of Jianguo Gate (*men*); Jianguomenwai refers to the area outside (*wai*) the gate.

Safety

You'll notice, once you've joined the masses at rush hour, there's a different concept of traffic etiquette than you may be accustomed to. In fact, some might claim there is no etiquette at all. The best rule in all cases is 'might makes right.' The bigger you are, the more right of way you have. This means you, as a lone rider on a two-wheeled vehicle, are near the bottom of the totem pole. Buses, trucks, cars, even presumptuous pedestrians, may plow right into your path. With all but the pedestrians, the principle is the same: clear out or be cleared.

As for the pedestrians, it appears they've not been taught to look before they cross. Don't imagine they'll suddenly find enlightenment. Give them a wide berth.

The second area of danger for a bicyclist in Beijing is of a stationary nature. At night especially, watch out for open manholes, potholes, and other obstacles along poorly lit roads. Broken glass, wire, all manner of debris, though rare on well-traveled city streets, do occasionally trip up the rider.

Bike safety in Beijing is a matter of both common sense (knowing your place and keeping your eyes open) and conforming to the rules. All major streets have bike lanes; many are protected from car traffic by a road divider. Though the temptation to break free from the crowd may be great, better keep inside these bike lanes where you belong. Intersections are usually provided with a traffic light or gesticulating traffic cop. Though many cyclers edge forward before the light turns green, better wait until it's your turn.

Take a lesson from the commuting Chinese: There's no hurry. The office isn't going anywhere, so you might as well enjoy the scenery along the way.

Background

History

Peking Man was among the first, some 500,000 years ago, to take up residence in the hills southwest of the present-day Chinese capital. Recorded history in this area began about 1,000 B.C., when Beijing served as a frontier trading town for the Mongols, Koreans, and other tribes from Shandong and central China. Though the town was headquarters for the Kingdom of Yan during the Warring States Period (476-221 B.C.), it wasn't until the tenth century that the city became capital for a more-or-less unified empire under the Khitan-based Liao Dynasty (916-1125). The earlier Han, Tang, and Song dynasties had all established capitals in central or eastern China.

Jurchen Tartars sacked the Liao in the twelfth century and set up their Jin Dynasty (1115- 1234) capital, Zhongdu (Central Metropolis), which subsequently burned to the ground in Genghis Khan's tour of destruction across the continent in 1215. Kublai Khan, his grandson, set the outlines of present-day Beijing during the Yuan Dynasty (1271-1368), calling his headquarters Dadu (Big Metropolis).

The next group in power, the Ming Dynasty (1368-1644), was of pure Han Chinese extraction. Though the founding emperor tried to move the capital south to Nanjing, his uppity son, Zhu Di (later Emperor Yongle), had migrated north to Beijing by 1420 after a seventeen-year urban renewal project. Many of the major structures, such as the Forbidden

City and the Temple of Heaven, as well as the overall city plan, date from this period.

Barbarians invaded from the north again in 1644, taking over the Chinese empire and establishing the Manchu Qing Dynasty (1644-1911). Emperors Kangxi and Qianlong in particular had temples, palaces, and gardens built at tremendous public expense for their private royal enjoyment. Though many of these structures were destroyed by western troops around the turn of the century, the Empress Dowager Cixi continued to rebuild through the dwindling days of the dynasty. The Republican Period (1911-1949) saw transfer of the capital to Nanjing by the Kuomintang in 1928, the Japanese occupation (1937-1945) and civil war, resulting in the victory of the People's Liberation Army (PLA) in 1949.

Declared once again the nation's capital, post-1949 Beijing has taken on a new look under Communist leadership. The city walls and commemorative arches were removed to clear the way for traffic and future development. In the fifties, first came the Stalinist blocks (the Great Hall of the People, Beijing Railway Station, the Friendship Hotel); in the sixties, cheap pre-fabricated housing and fallout shelters were constructed; by the eighties, there was a turn toward more innovative styles put up under joint-venture arrangements with foreign enterprises. The present development plan calls for less factories, more trees, wider roads, more suburban residential zones, and the preservation of old downtown districts.

Climate

Beijing revolves in seasons, each unfolding into the cityscape a new found aesthetic. Winter is the longest stretch of apparent consistency. From mid-November to mid-March, the city freezes into an endless block of bright, blustery days. (In recent years the temperature has rarely dropped below -12 degrees C.) The dry air, though good for visibility, is hard on the skin and lungs. Upper respiratory infections at this time of the year are common, due to the dryness and clouds of coal dust unleashed by furnaces city-wide.

Spring blows in for a short spell with dust storms in late March and April, then settles down to rejuvenate the city with budding trees of green and pink and yellow. May is a particularly delightful time to visit Beijing. By summer, the other season of some length, all is awash in green, the earth smells heavy and the sky, particularly in June, releases torrents of rain. July and August are insufferably hot (up to 38 degrees C), pierced by strong sunlight and riddled with mosquitoes. These are the best months, however, to enjoy local residents on parade.

Of all the seasons, the overwhelming favorite is autumn. From late-September through October, the skies hold blue. The days are generally warm and evenings cool. Summer's lush foliage mellows or brightens, decorating the city for a few fleeting weeks before the colors fade away.

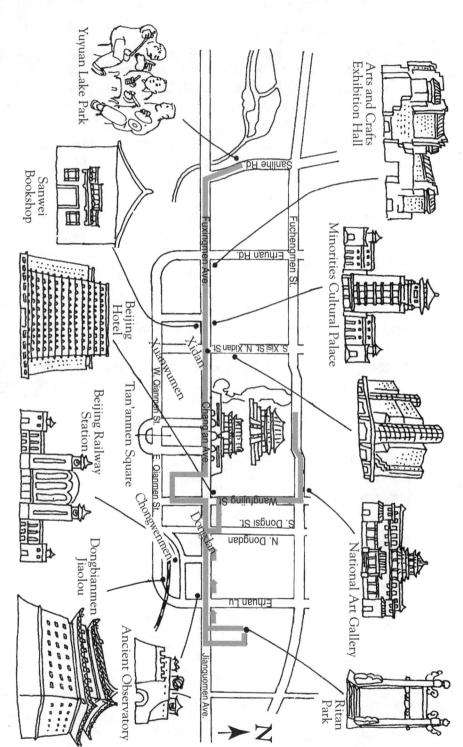

AUTUMN

The East-West Meridian

South along Sanlihe Road to Fuxingmen Avenue (Muxidi). East on Fuxingmen, along Chang'an Avenue through the city center (Tian'anmen) to Jianguomen Avenue in the east. North on Wangfujing, past the old lantern market street to the back of the Forbidden City.

In Season

Autumn slides in between wet layers of heat, slowly at first, so you barely notice it. But soon you will see the change in clothing styles. People wear cotton tank tops (a rainbow of vibrant colors on the chests of manual laborers) and plain, nearly transparent short-sleeved shirts (the white of the white-collar class, known in China as "intellectuals"). In the evening long sleeves, knit vests, and light sweaters appear. Autumn slows the whir of the summer cicada in the parasol tree and sends shouting parades of children past my window home for lunch. Autumn brings crisp green mountain apples, plump rosy grapes, and mushy orange persimmons. Autumn paints the last strokes of color before the city drops its leaves and takes a prolonged winter nap.

Autumn is clearly the best season in Beijing. It is the best time for a sister and her friend to visit from the States, and the best time to take a day off from work to tour around the city by bike.

The three of us—Jan, Erron, and I—dressed in shorts and sweat shirts. We stuffed our packs with wind breakers, obligatory bottles of water, and apples. Our plan was to make a longitudinal tour, following Chang'an Avenue (Avenue of Eternal Peace; the main thoroughfare cutting through the city's southern heart) from west to east. The ride straight through at a moderate clip takes only thirty minutes, twenty if you race. But we planned to fill the day, leaving ourselves open to detours and photo opportunities.

Jade Lake Park

Southward along Sanlihe Road, we came to the **Jade Lake Park** (*Yuyuan*) entrance. Jade Lake Park is the site of the local swimming hole. The shallow lake in back is designated for swimming, but old-timers (and some new) ignore the "no swimming" notice and stick devoutly to the deeper, wider, all around preferable, front lake. Rumor has it that the local swimming hole is also our water supply, which is probably why they'd like us to keep out.

Skaters take over in the winter, though a small square is cut in the ice to one side for the stout of heart, those who enjoy an invigorating dip in below freezing water. Adherents of the sport seem to fall into one of two categories: rotund, crazy, middle-aged men, and rotund, crazy, old-aged men. Preparation for the plunge requires the emission of several loud, sharp cries in rapid succession. The ritual is repeated after the exercise has been completed. Then the ice-swimmer bicycles home, unnaturally warm in the freezing air.

Jade Lake was relocated here in 1956 from its original spot in the **Angler's Terrace** (*Diaoyutai*) parkland. Water from the Yongding River feeds through it to the former moat arcing a southern circle around the city. Angler's Terrace is now known for its state guesthouse, where long black limousines cruise in past the heavily guarded gate, and guests are rumored to have free run of the fish ponds. The gardens and halls are reputed to be superb; deluxe suites in the diplomatic residential complex may be booked through the **China International Travel Service** (CITS) for a cool $200 U.S. and up.

There is a story about this area—a fish story—that comes from the twelfth century. It tells of a Jin Dynasty official, seeking refuge from court life, who secluded himself on one of the lakeside terraces in the disguise of a fisherman. The area eventually became home to nobility through the dynasties. The dilapidated Angler's Terrace fell into the busy hands of Emperor Qianlong of the Qing Dynasty, who got to work on repairs mid-way through his career. First he dredged the lake and filled it with spring water from the Fragrant Hills. Next he built a traveling lodge that was ready for enjoyment by 1773.

Singers and Dancers

The sidewalk before the **Jade Lake Park** (*Yuyuan*) entrance was thronged with outdoor barbers clipping in the shade. From behind a screen of shrubbery came the wails and crashes of a morning operatic gathering

There's nothing quite like coming upon a group of old men, in parks or temples, from morning to afternoon, bellowing out their favorite Beijing opera tunes to the plucks and whines of age-old instruments.

We stopped to tunnel our way through the bushes. A dozen of them had congregated under a roof of trailing wisteria—round, thin, tall, bent—all dressed in somber blues and grays, singularly concentrated on the singer's pitch and roll. So concentrated, in fact, no one blinked an eye in our direction.

Jan pulled out her camera and aimed it at the lead singer. Still no one blinked. She stepped over the low concrete seat that acted as a boundary between performers and audience for a close-up of his whiskered, delicately-carved face.

Our singer straightened his shoulders with a twist of the head, poised carefully on the balls of his feet, and raised his eyebrows in proper Beijing opera style. Erron leaped into the inner circle. The posing and eyebrow raising and grimacing went on for some time before I was able to extricate my happy photographers. We repeated our thanks *"xie-xie, xie-xie"* and goodbyes *"zai-jian, zai-jian,"* while backing slowly out of the circle.

Chinese chess games were in progress nearby. Loose circles of onlookers studied the boards, smoking with an intensity unmatched by the contestants themselves. Bamboo-caged birds hung in the pines, chattering insistently over the music. Opera, chess, birds—this was a man's world, these the hobbies of the retired working man. Only a few women lingered on the edges.

Most of the grandmothers who'd come out that fine morning were "dancing" in singles and pairs to taped music on the wide flagstone drive leading into the park. Another dozen were practicing sword play or doing breathing exercises under the trees. The rest were probably at home watching the grandkids or out doing the day's shopping.

The Fuxingmen Stretch

Jan and Erron turned their cameras next on the white-coated barbers scattering tufts of black hair over the pavement. Their victims smiled courageously at us. What can you expect from a one *yuan* haircut?

We finally pushed off, turned left at Muxidi (not to be confused with Mushu Pork) and dove into the great stream of bicycles on Fuxingmen Avenue (which becomes Chang'an Avenue toward the center of the city). This street always seems crowded. It is six lanes across, including the bike lanes. Riding along you get the extravagant feeling that you can go all day without getting anywhere. The **Military Museum** west of Muxidi, with its pictures of Mao and instruments of destruction, held a five-pointed star to the blue sky at our backs.

The stretch from Muxidi to the subway stop at Fuxingmen holds nothing of particular interest, save for the **Yanjing Hotel** and a new razzle-dazzle department store known as the **Chang'an Market**. Shoppers flock there in summer to enjoy the atmosphere. Central air-conditioning in some of these stores is about the best advertisement going.

We cruised past the radio broadcasting tower at the corner of the Fuxingmen overpass. Headquarters for "Radio Beijing," China's answer to BBC, VOA, and other internationally-broadcast government stations, the Stalinesque block sits squarely inside a walled compound. Its busy workers, including foreign staff, put out a daily program in thirty-eight different languages.

Across the Second Ring Road (*Erhuan Lu*), in startling contrast to the radio complex, rises the shiny **Arts and Crafts Exhibition Hall**, boldly crafted of broad angles, white marble, and reflective glass. After the rush of curious crowds at its grand opening in 1989, the place seems to have dipped into hibernation. Special exhibits and seasonal garment fairs are held here.

Directly east of the exhibition hall is China International Travel Service (CITS). Their smiling staff has been specially trained to deal with the international set. Plans and problems are their forte.

Next along the northern side of Chang'an is the **People's Bank of China**. The newly completed facility, a circular gray affair with the bank's name in burnished gold, appears to have recently dropped in from outer space. Post-economic reform architecture in Beijing gleams with the very individualism that the Soviet-inspired monoliths of the fifties insisted upon rubbing out.

A little further on, also to the north, are the **Minorities Hotel** (*Minzu Fandian*) and the **Minorities Cultural Palace** (*Minzu Gong*), a green-roofed, museum-library-auditorium combo built in the shape of the Chinese character for "mountain." The two bronze doors in front of the palace announce in bold characters the official policy for dealing with minority groups: "Solidarity" and "Progress." (Han Chinese, the ethnic majority, make up 93% of the country's population. There are fifty-five other ethnic groups within the country's borders.)

The museum occasionally runs a decent temporary exhibit. Sometimes local photographers and artists show their works here or in the smaller show rooms underground. It's all a matter of scouting them out.

Three Flavors

The **Three Flavors** (*Sanwei*) Bookshop is located directly across the street from the Minorities Palace. Recently released from years of confinement behind blue metal siding (for construction of the Xidan subway stop), the house of three flavors is looking sharper than ever in a coat of white paint and freshly stained wood trimming.

Sanwei is a small shop with a personal touch. The tables stacked with magazines and newspapers, the friendly staff, the plants and easy atmosphere will not strike the newcomer to China as unusual. But for those who make Beijing their home, it's a jewel among rough-cut stones. Unlike most state bookstores, where clerks suffer from sight and hearing disorders (while miraculously able to engage in animated conversation with their co-workers), the salespeople at Sanwei ask "What can I do for you?" "What is it you're looking for?" These small pleasantries pass by the overindulged, but are hoarded by the starved.

On the second floor comes another welcome surprise—an airy, tastefully decorated teahouse. Dark wood chairs and tables, reminiscent of centuries past, draw from the walls the dramatic flourishes of modern Chinese paintings. Here is a place to sit over a cup of tea, contemplating art, discussing politics, writing poetry.... Open every day until 11 pm, the teahouse provides a pleasant respite from Beijing's crowded streets and a chance to meet some interesting personalities.

We stopped outside the shop to pull off our sweatshirts to the undisguised amazement of the construction workers shuffling by at that opportune moment. I wondered, was it our arms, ridiculously bare when most Chinese were already beginning to layer themselves against winter, that caught the eye of the jacketed gang? Probably not. We are a spectacle in and of ourselves (big noses, blue eyes, yellow hair). Anything we *do* is an encore to an already riveting performance. In China you can experience all the thrills and pitfalls of celebrity-hood.

Our next destination was Xidan, only a few hundred meters ahead. We wheeled our bikes along the leafy sidewalk. The low gray wall to the south was dotted with older couples folded like blue sofa cushions along the edge of the flower planters. Some grandpas leaned against the trees smoking. Some strolled in the shade, grandchildren bouncing beside them. Across the whirring, grinding avenue of Eternal Peace towered the imposing giants of modern urban development.

It is difficult to avoid the city-of-contrasts, a cliché engendered in the drive toward modernization. While Beijing tries to "catch up" with the rest of the world, building ever taller buildings, clearing the way for the newer, the bigger, the brighter, some old remnants of the past still hang on.

The Lean

The smattering of restaurants and shops explodes suddenly into mass commotion at the crossroads of North Xidan Street. Negotiating a left-hand turn through the stream of buses and taxis on Chang'an can be a tricky affair for first-timers. Insulated by a pack of like-minded riders, we crossed safely and turned northward.

We rode single file—the first time that day—to work our way through the traffic. Dodge the old man. Swerve around the three-wheeler. Don't brush too close or you'll lock handlebars and find yourself on the ground. Jan and Erron are both experienced bicyclists, having lived for years in Davis, California, the state's "bike capital." But speeding down a secluded bike path on a light-footed racing machine is no preparation for squeezing between a trundling trolleybus and wall of spinning wheels. Balance and timing are essential.

Pulling off the street in front of the **Xidan Market**, we located a bike lot near the pedestrian overpass. Bike lots can be desperately jammed, pedal to spoke, handlebar to frame. As he threaded his bicycle into an impossible slot, the pedal on Erron's bike caught in the spokes of its neighbor. He pulled back, too abruptly, throwing the culprit off balance and pushing the entire line-up to one side. Slowly the tilt began. But as in a packed bus where passengers *lean* rather than fall, they *leaned* persuasively to the right without uttering a clatter. An experienced attendant caught the lean mid-flow with a cheerful explosion of profanity, righted the line with a push, and waved us on our way, probably hoping to avoid more foreigner-induced disasters.

Xidan

The **Xidan Market** is one of the most fashionable spots this side of town. The place intrigues me, though the source of my fascination was of questionable interest to my guests, who could not appreciate the recent deluge of western (particularly American) products at prohibitively marked-up prices.

Who buys that pound of Kraft Cheese Whiz for thirty-two *yuan* (over five dollars)? Or that Skippy peanut butter for twenty-seven, when the local brand, without all those preservatives, goes for three? Who buys that Chivas Regal Scotch Whiskey at 280 *yuan*, which is more than an average worker's monthly salary plus bonus, or those mini-bottles of airplane liquor for twelve to twenty-eight? The international crowd doesn't frequent this place. They have their own shops on the other side of town. There are plenty of well-dressed lookers (which means little because many Beijingers would rather wear their money than eat it) but few takers.

Up an escalator, we stopped to try on the long black wigs (worthy of a gaping crowd in China) and play the electric organs (another crowd) in the toy department. Upstairs looks like the high-fashion end of an American shopping mall. But each store sells only the brand of its parent company (try on "Flying Phoenix" sports jackets or "Double Lucky" fur coats for size).

Jan and Erron were wearing thin with the crowds. I suggested we get a bite to eat and led them to a Sichuan-style snack house near the corner of Chang'an Avenue. **Tianfu Douhua Zhuang** (*Tianfu*, "land of abundance," refers to the agriculturally-rich Sichuan Province; *Douhua Zhuang* means "Tofu Village") is easy to spot by its raised, double-sided entrance under an arching roof on the east side of the street.

We made our selections from the brewing pots, bought tickets from the cashier, and carried our bowls to a cramped table. The self-serve system is easy if you know Chinese, doable without. All the choices of noodles, boiled tofu with sauce, won-ton, skewered meat or mushrooms, pickled vegetables, and sweet dumplings are within pointing range. The food is tasty and cheap—nothing over three *yuan* for the snacks downstairs, though a full menu of Sichuan dishes is available on the second floor.

Everything comes with hot sauce, the signature of Sichuan food. You can, however, specify without and get dishes with less flavor. (In that case, why go to a Sichuan-style restaurant?) Mouths burning, we walked next door to **Charlie's Ice Cream** for a couple of cool scoops.

Avenue of Eternal Peace

We were soon back into the main stream on West Chang'an Avenue. From a bicyclist's point of view, one important advantage major boulevards offer over the more flavorful alleyways are partitioned bike lanes. A concrete island separates the rider from the motorized hoard. The only drawback is that buses pick up and drop off passengers from the island. Waves of recently disembarked passengers flow fearlessly, without looking, across the bike path toward the sidewalk.

The normal pedestrian strategy is to proceed as if no one else exists. Cross without looking; others will do that for you. This inspired philosophy turns the road into a minefield for the bicyclist. Who knows when someone's going to step off the curb directly into your path? Or halt mid-step to reflect upon their plans for the day? Be ready for anything, and keep your fingers to the brake.

We rode past the spanking new **China Airlines** headquarters and the decades old **Telegraph Office**, both on the left. Here the scenery begins to change. Six lanes widens to eight. A forbidding red wall dominates the north. Traffic police raise their chins a notch higher. We were passing in front of the Zhongnanhai

Compound, headquarters of China's top leadership, Beijing's new forbidden city.

Central and South Lakes (*Zhongnanhai*) was cultivated as an imperial pleasure park in the Liao Dynasty, and maintained as such right up through the last imperial years. Emperor Guangxu of the Qing Dynasty was locked up on the South Lake Island (when he wasn't being kept behind bricks at the Summer Palace). Yuan Shikai, the new president of the Chinese republic, moved his government here in 1912. In one form or another, it's remained the seat of power in China ever since. The highest-ranking members of the Communist Party (Mao Zedong, Zhou Enlai, Liu Shaoqi, and Zhu De, among others) have lived and worked—still live and work—behind these walls.

Chang'an Avenue was opened to the public in 1912 after more than five hundred years of restricted use. During the Ming Dynasty, both the square (a narrow T-shaped corridor in those days) and the entire length of road stretching from Xidan in the west to Dongdan in the east were off-limits to commoners. Only the top three scholars in the triennial imperial examinations were allowed, after receiving their titles, to ride out from the Gate of Heavenly Peace (*Tian'anmen*) along this road to the celebratory feast.

A mere seven meters wide at its turn-of-the-century public debut, the avenue now balloons a full ten lanes across, with room to spare for the critical Tian'anmen Square approach. For the first time that day, space ranged in excess.

The Square

Everyone who comes to Beijing aspires to visit **Tian'anmen Square**. And not without reason. Though

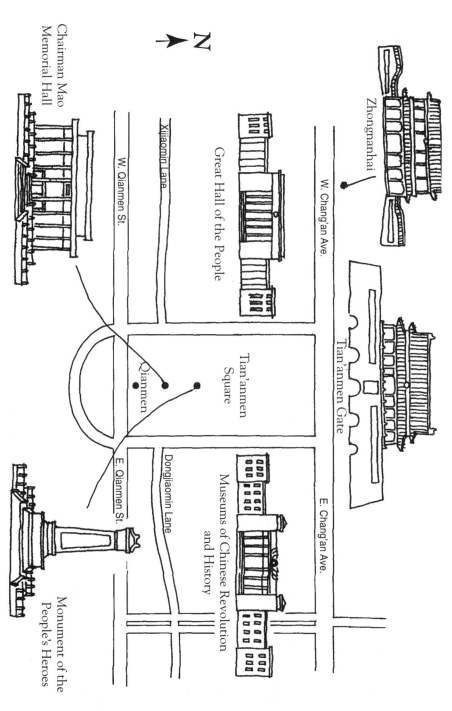

drawn in a heavy, severe hand, the lines exude a bold, self-righteous claim to national dignity. Host to numerous anti-imperialist, patriotic demonstrations in the pre-1949 era, the square in its new enlarged form remains, both symbolically and in practice, the rallying point for the expression of dissatisfaction with government policies. Reputed to be the largest urban plaza in the world, the Square has a standing capacity of 500,000, each person occupying a single checkerboard stone.

Things were very different, however, before 1949. Imagine gazing south from Tian'anmen Gate and seeing not the square and its colossal buildings, but a smallish plaza leading to a roofed corridor. To each side sat numerous medium-sized halls. During the Ming and Qing dynasties, the principal organs of government established their offices here: to the east, the Boards of Ceremonies, Finance, War, Works, Personnel, Meteorology, and Astronomy; to the west, the five military commissions. The "Thousand *Bu* Corridor," so named for the number of steps (measured at about five feet) required to walk from one end to the next, drew the line between the civil and military authorities.

The Square is bounded on four sides by four tremendous structures: Tian'anmen Gate to the north, with the Forbidden City behind (see *What to See* for more information on the Forbidden City); **The Great Hall of the People** to the west; The Museum of Chinese History and Chinese Revolution to the east; and the Chairman Mao Memorial Hall to the south.

The Great Hall of the People is indeed great. It has a total floor space of 171,000 square meters. It's actually the great hall of congress—for the Party and government, as well as the reception quarters for foreign heads of state—but the people are welcome in for a look when the leaders aren't in session. There's a 5,000 seat banquet hall—where Nixon dined in 1972—and a modern auditorium that can seat 10,000. We passed by its grand front entrance, lined by pines and an occasional green uniformed PLA (People's Liberation Army) man, and came out upon the vast desert of sky and flagstone that is Tian'anmen Square.

Parking in the area is a dubious event, usually up to the whim of the guards on duty. We stuck our bikes in with a few scattered near the Great Hall, hoping the PLA men wouldn't notice, and crossed over into the Square. Fair weather had called out a substantial crowd that day. Chinese tourists milled about, posing and snapping pictures, pointing and chatting. Most hung near the northern edge, where every Chinese who's made it to the big city gets their picture taken with **Tian'anmen Gate** and the Mao Zedong portrait as backdrop (the same spot was formerly occupied by pictures of Sun Yat-sen and Chiang Kaishek). Foreign tourists also milled around, aiming video cameras at themselves and the Chinese. Paper kites wheeled in the blue sky above.

The Gate

We stood for awhile by the picture-takers to get a good look at the gate from which Mao Zedong proclaimed a new China on October 1, 1949 to an audience of 500,000 (every checkerboard stone was taken that day). Built in the fifteenth century during the Ming Dynasty, it burned when the Manchus stormed into town. It was reconstructed in the seventeenth century for the new Qing Dynasty (ruled by the Manchus). There are five entryways and seven bridges, each of which enjoyed designated use in imperial days. The widest bridge, in the middle, was reserved strictly for the emperor (and the men below who bore his sedan chair).

A royal palace exit was nothing to blink at. The roads were first prepared with a sprinkling of water and a layer of yellow earth. Then thousands upon thousands of officials and attendants came out to line the intended route and accompany the emperor in his dragon robes and golden crown.

The crimson grandstands flanking the gate seat 20,000. A post-1949 addition, they would have been useful in imperial days, when other exciting events included imperial exam parties; bloody, randomly determined trials of accused prisoners; and the enthronement of emperors. Now the biggest show here is the National Day extravaganza on October 1. The slogans "Long Live the People's Republic of China" to the left and "Long Live the Unity of the Peoples of the World" to the right are also post-1949 improvements.

Memorials

Turning southward, we faced the ten-story marble and granite **Monument to the People's Heroes**, and the **Chairman Mao Memorial Hall** across the square. Mao died in 1976 and has been kept, embalmed, in this hall ever since. We checked our packs at the left luggage booth (no bags or cameras allowed inside) and joined the lines of visitors awaiting admittance.

Inside, we trod silently over the thick-pile red carpet past a white marble statue of the late chairman. His crystal casket lies in the inner sanctuary. Word has it he's lowered into the ground to sleep out the colder months and off-duty hours. There are some exhibits on other greats in Chinese Communist history—Zhou Enlai, Zhu De, Liu Shaoqi—as well as the toothbrush and towel Mao used when the Party was camped out in Yenan to complete the tour.

Behind the mausoleum stand two large city gates, collectively known as **Qianmen** (Front Gate). The southernmost structure is the **Arrow Tower** (*Jian Lou*), reconstructed in 1903 from the design of a German architect. To the north is the **Gate Facing the Sun** (*Zhengyangmen*). Up until the 1950s, a twenty-meter-thick stone wall connected this central entrance with two other gates, Chongwenmen to the east and Xuanwumen to the west. Of the three, Qianmen remains the sole reminder of the days when gates were locked and the city closed off at night. Its flanking partners, having met the same fate as the Inner City wall, are now only street corners and subway stops. The small square between us and Qianmen was in former days a busy hub of commerce known as Chessboard Street.

We retrieved our packs and bikes and were on our way. Looping around the southern edge of the square, we passed the top of Qianmen Street, the "entertainment" hot-spot in imperial days and now one of Beijing's busiest commercial districts (see the *Spring* section for more on this area). China's first Kentucky Fried Chicken outlet, one of four in the capital and the largest in the world, towers in red and white over the noisy ring of snack booths below.

Museums

We turned north to pick up Chang'an Avenue and passed the **History Museum** on our right. Housed in a somber building, the museum distinguishes between

History (from Day One to 1919) and Revolution (from 1919 to 1949, when China was liberated by the Communist Party). The history side is packed with bronze ware, pottery, art objects, weapons, inventions, and musical instruments. Revolution is preserved with documents and pictures of the Party's first thirty years. Torches carved on the front pylons eternalize Mao's idea that, "a single spark can start a prairie fire."

Eastward again on Chang'an Avenue, we passed the **Working People's Cultural Palace**. In colloquial English that means: public park for cultural activities—sports, theater, cinema, exhibitions, and fairs. In the old days it was the site of the Imperial Ancestral Temple (*Taimiao*), the memorial tablet repository for the emperors' forebearers.

Behind us on the west side of Tian'anmen Gate lay **Zhongshan Park**, a memorial to Sun Yat-sen. Formerly the Altar of Land and Grain, it is now a spread of trees and flowers dedicated to the "Father of the Country." Some of the huge cypresses here are said to have been planted about a thousand years ago during the Liao Dynasty.

Foreign Fortress

The large rectangle of land from Tian'anmen all the way to Dongdan Street in the east is packed with history. The story begins in the late thirteenth century, when the Grand Canal was connected to the urban waterways of the Yuan Dynasty capital to facilitate rice and textile shipments from the south. A rice market grew up in this area, lending the name East Glutinous Rice Lane to the main east-west thoroughfare. In 1416, the Ming Emperor Yongle decreed that the space was to be kept free for raising animals and growing crops. But by the late Ming and early Qing dynasties, the Six Boards, or ministries, of the imperial government had already moved in and set up office.

In 1727, the Russians were the first foreigners to establish an embassy in this quarter. They were followed more than a century later by France and Great Britain, who moved in after their troops destroyed Yuanmingyuan (the old Summer Palace) in 1861.

It was in 1901, however, that the **Legation Quarter** took on a new look. In the year previous, the Boxers (a peasant secret society known also as the "Righteous and Harmonious Fists"), supported by the Qing court, began to attack all forms of Western influence in the capital and beyond. Reinforced by regular troops, they held some 900 foreigners and 2,300 Chinese Christians under siege for fifty-five days. Harsh retaliation by the Western powers led to the signing of the Boxer Protocol, which gave foreign governments the right to station their own troops and establish legations in the capital.

A wall was put up around the quarter, and the open grounds outside were reserved for foreign military exercises and polo. The British barracks oversaw the northern gate (present site of the History Museum). American troops guarded the west (across from Qianmen). East Glutinous Rice Lane, ironically renamed East Intercourse with the People Lane (*Dongjiaomin*) during the late Qing Dynasty, was thereby proclaimed off-limits to Chinese citizens. The wall and foreign sentries saw to it that no one "trespassed."

This invaders' outpost remained under foreign jurisdiction until the Communists came to power in 1949. Most Western countries then moved their embassies to Taiwan, leaving Legation Street to countries loyal to mainland China: Bulgaria, Hungary, Burma,

East Germany, and India. The Soviets moved north to the grounds of the former Russian Church mission, an enormous plot of land now occupied by the representative Russian Embassy.

Returning from their Taiwan sojourn in the 1970s, Western countries were allocated housing in either Jianguomen or Sanlitun, the capital's two modern diplomatic compounds.

Beijing's Little Europe

The former Legation Quarter (Dongjiaomin Lane) is often glossed over in guidebooks. In fact, it houses a wealth of government organizations, including the Beijing Municipal People's Government, the Fire Department, the Beijing Public Security Bureau, the High Court, and the Association for Friendship with Foreign Countries. The meeting ground of old, new, and rehabilitated buildings, it's the perfect place for a self-guided walking or biking tour.

We turned right off Chang'an Avenue into Zhengyi Road. Foreign residents used to call it Canal Street because a canal—now a shady park down the middle—ran water up to Zhongnanhai. To the right are the former British and Russian legations. The Russian quarter is now occupied by China's High Court. To the left are the former Italian and Japanese legations, home now to the Beijing Municipal People's Government.

Dongjiaomin Lane takes you straight to the heart of the old neighborhood. We turned right by a small fruit market to explore the western end. A few of the old structures remain—a heavy columned bank, the squarish Dutch residence, and a brick building trimmed with wrought iron window-work. The former

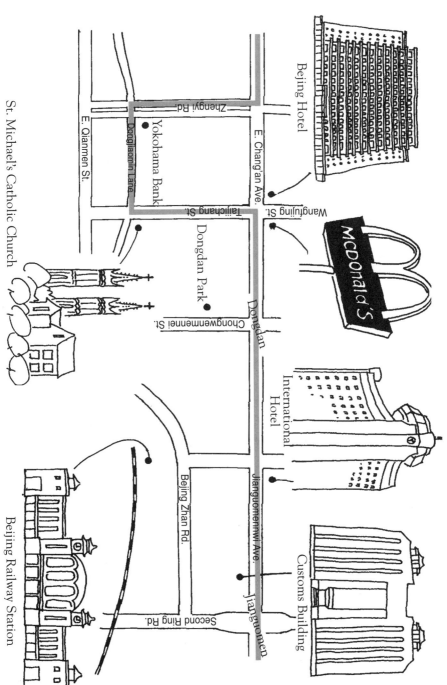

American legation in the far west, now the property of the People's Court, is vintage 1901, having been rebuilt after the attack of the Boxers. The oldest remaining structures all date from that time.

Doubling back, we stopped at the market across from the Yokohama Bank (now a Chinese finance company) for baked sweet potatoes fresh from the coals. One of old Beijing's most famous hotels, the Grand Hotel des Wagons-Lits, once occupied the southern corner. Looking up, we surveyed the historical record: a crazy hodgepodge of glassy skyscrapers, red brick and carved stone.

The imposing gate guarded by young lions and stone soldiers on the corner of Taijichang Street (Marco Polo Street) and Dongjiaomin Lane opens into the former French legation, now a sumptuous state guesthouse. Like the former British legation, this compound was home to a Manchu prince in the 1860s before financial trouble forced him to rent it to the foreigners. The solid red house in the former Belgian compound to the south, on the other hand, is an authentic import. It was modeled after a villa in Brussels that belonged to King Leopold II. **St. Michael's Catholic Church** across the way, built by the French in 1902, still holds Sunday services under its spire.

Grand Hotel de Pekin

Emerging from the former Legation Quarter at Wangfujing Street, we found ourselves face-to-face with the Beijing Hotel. The original **Grand Hotel de Pekin** was built in 1917 with money from the Sino-French Bank of Industry and Commerce. Catering to the foreign crowd, it was French-managed until 1940, when the Japanese bought up most of the shares and renamed it the Japan Club that lasted only until 1945. The new Grand Hotel, at the far western end of the long block, has been recently renovated in ultra-deluxe style.

The Beijing Hotel used to be *the* place in town, a watering hole for journalists, students, tourists, and business people from all over the world. That's changed in the last ten years with the joint-venture hotel boom and an exploding number of other likely social spots. The Great Wall Sheraton, the Jianguo Hotel, and the Holiday Inn were some of the first big names to break in on the action. Now the list of five-star hotels goes on and on. They keep popping up like rice sprouts, especially in the Chaoyang District.

The other mentionable at that corner is a newly installed McDonald's Restaurant. Don't come to Beijing with romantic notions of sloped tile roofs, fried rice, and the pat-pat of a rickshaw boy's feet on flagstone. Do come expecting to meet Ronnie perched up against the sky, beckoning you in for a hamburger, shake, and fries. The temptation of familiarity has softened more than one self-acclaimed purist. How many times have I heard, "You'd never catch me in a McDonald's back home."

We merged eastward into the stream of bicycles on Chang'an Avenue. Across the street behind McDonald's is the walkway, relatively quiet during daylight hours, that perks up when the sun begins to slide. It's one of the night markets in Wangfujing—a good place to look around if you're hankering for something to eat, but don't know quite what it is you want. They've got all manner of steamed, boiled, and fried—especially fried—noodles, buns, and meat—especially meat. A carnival of delights for the carnivorous.

Train Station Country

Caught by a red light at the Dongdan intersection, we pulled up behind a couple of long-bed, three-wheeled bike carts. The special gear on these vehicles makes it possible for them to haul large, heavy loads; lack of decent brakes facilitates wild careening through the alleys.

Two lean and dusty cart drivers carried on a lively conversation in some unintelligible, out-of-town dialect. Dressed in blue cotton jackets, patched at the elbow, and black cloth shoes worn thin, their haul consisted of fresh bokchoy and lettuce covered by a burlap sack. To their left, foot propped up on the street divider to avoid a full dismount, a young hotshot in stone washed jeans and maroon silk jacket slouched over his purple mountain bike.

The light turned green, our traffic cop waved, and we were off. The mountain bike jumped to an early lead but was followed close behind by a black cruiser. I darted around the carts, pumping hard to keep pace, but then remembered Jan and Erron. Looking around, I spotted them pushing on steadily behind the dusty drivers. Recalling my duties, I reluctantly shifted down to tour guide speed and waited for them to catch up.

The next block is train-station country. Already we were confronted with a dazed crew of out-of-town gawkers shuffling across the bike lane. I frantically thumbed my bell to clear the way, but the polite "ding-ding" did as much good as asking an elephant to kindly step aside. Jan squeaked on her brakes to let the mob pass, and they pushed on, mouths gaping at the blue-eyed wonder.

South of the next intersection looms the **Beijing Railway Station** (*Beijing Zhan*). One of three railway terminals in the city, Beijing Zhan is the most popular and well-loved among western travelers. All of us have had our day to weave through the jungle of waiting bodies strewn over the front plaza, edge around the congestion at baggage inspection, and hop over cloth sacks in the main vestibule to line up in the "Foreigners' Booking Office" for a ticket out of town. Too often, something goes wrong. Insufficient supply and ticket seller obstinacy greatly reduce chances for a one-shot purchase. Then it's back over the sacks, through the lines, and around the bodies...to repeat the process the next day.

For the Chinese sitting on the ground, however, buying tickets is an ordeal unimagined by pampered western tourists. They get to spend hours packed in an airless, buzzing room, standing then crouching, crouching then standing, smoking and sighing, until finally a voice snarls through the money-hole "closed!" and "whack" the money-hole snaps shut. And to repeat the process the next day.

The block leading to the station was once lined with shops selling train supplies—cigarettes, edibles, and drinkables (the hard stuff for hard-seat journeys), batteries, toilet paper, and silverware. They've since been cleared to make way for shopping centers catering to a new generation of travelers.

Managing Heaven

Straight on east we came to the Jianguomen traffic circle. Just behind the mouth of the subway sits another reminder of the past among the forest of high-rises. The **Ancient Observatory**, mounted on the battlements of the former city wall watchtower, was once the center of astrological activity in the Chinese capital. When Kublai Khan hit upon the idea of an observa-

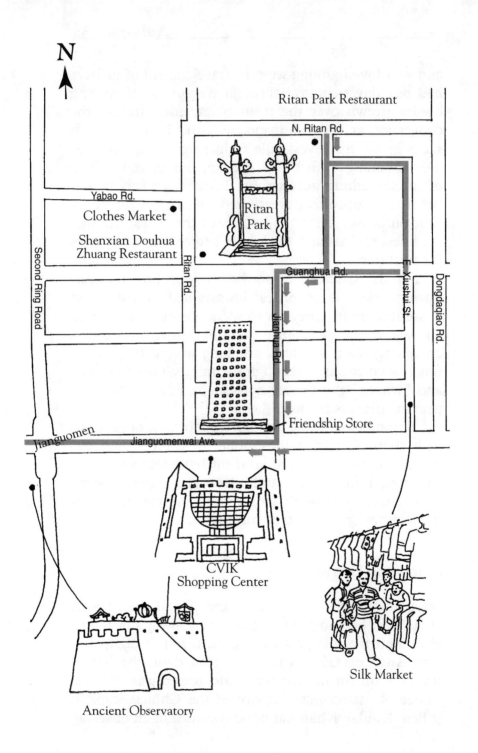

ANCIENT OBSERVATORY TO SILK ALLEY

tory, he built his modest "Terrace for Managing Heaven" somewhat north of its present location.

The small gray fortress we see today took over "Managing Heaven" in the middle years of the Ming Dynasty. Here the stars were observed and mapped, astrological predictions made, and sea navigation planned. Displays in the museum inside are from that era. They include navigational equipment and roof tiles designating direction. There is also a celestial map dating from the Tang Dynasty.

The Jesuits, led by Matteo Ricci in the early fifteenth century, pushed the study of heaven far beyond those first crude maps. Having proven themselves to the emperor, the Jesuits were given control of the observatory and, as official court advisors, became China's first "foreign experts."

Six of the eight bronze astronomical instruments on the roof were designed and constructed under the supervision of a Belgian priest. Though cleverly embellished with sculpted bronze dragons and other Chinese decorations, French and German forces must have mistaken the bronze pieces for their own toys. They looted the observatory after the Boxer Rebellion of 1900 and only returned their prizes when forced to do so by the Treaty of Versailles in 1919. The Ancient Observatory is open every day except Monday, 9 to 11 am and 1 to 4 pm.

Another World

Moving into the eastern district outside the subway demarcation line, things begin to change. This is embassy land, foreign company land, airline office land, imported goods land, and black market land. There are two embassy neighborhoods: Jianguomen, in the south near Ritan Park, and Sanlitun, further north near the Worker's Stadium. They and the foreign companies and news agencies centralized in this area supply a diversity of skin tone and language that create a surprisingly cosmopolitan atmosphere.

The drag from the Jianguomen traffic circle on the Second Ring Road to the sparkling China World Trade Center on the Third Ring Road is littered with high-rise hotels, higher-rise office buildings, and fancy shopping opportunities. Slipping through the web of bikes circling willfully against the flow of traffic, we passed the Hotel New Otani, a recent Japanese investment of little aesthetic value. Across the way, on the north, is a balcony-lined embassy housing complex. The balconies' only benefit, judging by the lack of sunbathers, is easy access to car exhaust and traffic rumble from below.

Next door to the embassy apartments is the International Club, a state-run facility for the international jet-set. Its amenities include gift shops, a Japanese steak restaurant, hair salon, video library, and tennis courts. The black CITIC (China International Trade and Investment Corporation; pronounced "si-tick" by the locals) building, one of the first office-space towers in the city allowed to foreign companies, is a reliable landmark. The Kodak photo processing lab on the first floor is a landmark, too, in its own right. They don't scratch up negatives as do many places in town.

Shopper Friendly

Crossing the street by "Uncle Sam's" fast food joint, we cut through the CITIC parking lot to the Friendship Store. Everybody who comes to Beijing, whether on a guided tour or spontaneous adventure, stops at least once at the **Friendship Store**. It's certainly one of the most comfortable and complete ways to get through a gift list. Many of the items are unavailable elsewhere in China. They have everything from carpets to cloisonné, pottery to pastry. They even take care of packing, customs, and shipping. You do pay for the convenience, however. For those with more time and less money, the International Post Office is tucked around the corner to the north on the Second Ring Road.

In the old days, before the advent of free markets, foreign residents had to rely on the Friendship Store for daily necessities. Oil, flour, rice, sugar, meat, and eggs were unattainable without ration coupons; quality fruit and vegetables were hard to come by. A freer market system has now opened up a new phase of consumerism in China. Nearly everything (including imported luxury items) can be bought at competitive prices in local shops and outdoor farmers' markets. The Friendship Store still serves many of the nutritional needs of the east-town international crowd, who, though often linguistically equipped to deal in the markets, prefer the one-stop supermarket shopping in a dust-free environment.

Jan had been talking about buying a pig-suede backpack. Up in the leather department on the second floor they have everything—hats, jackets, bags, belts, wallets—everything you can stitch up from a piece of animal skin. As in most stores in China, all is stored safely behind the glass counter. Jan had to ask several times to get the one she wanted.

The clothes, shoes, and linens upstairs used to be rare luxury items, but over the past ten years the influx of foreign capital and standards have exploded the fashion market in Beijing. There are now shops and stalls all over town that deal in export-quality wear.

Temple of the Sun

Collecting our bicycles from the bike man at the corner, we turned north along the embassy lane toward **Temple of the Sun Park** (*Ritan*). Ritan was once the site of an imperial sacrificial altar, like the **Temple of Heaven** (*Tiantan*) to the south. Emperors during the Ming and Qing dynasties, in accordance with established rites, relinquished the luxurious confines of home to make regular sacrifices to the sun, moon, earth, heaven, and gods at altars laid out in a rough circle around the Forbidden City. At the winter solstice, it was down to the Temple of Heaven (see the *Spring* section for a description of the rites). In the second month, it was to the Temple of the God of Agriculture to plow a couple furrows in the sacred field. At the summer solstice, it was up to the Temple of the Earth. And so on around the capital.

At Ritan, only the ruins of the altar (built in 1530) remain. It is as much a nice park with a couple decent restaurants as it is a cultural landmark. In the spring, flowers amass and color; in the fall, trees take over with brilliant reds and yellows.

Both well-established eateries at opposite corners of the park offer reasonable dishes and spacious outdoor seating. In the southwest, **Shenxian Douhua Zhuang** (of the same fame as the Xidan Sichuan-style snack house we'd visited that morning) provides menus in English accompanied by a three-piece Chinese music ensemble when the weather's fair. We cycled around to the **Ritan Park Restaurant** in the northeast. The dishes were nothing special—the usual selection of stir-fried meat and vegetables—but the *jiaozi* (boiled dumplings) and sunny, open courtyard made for an excellent late lunch.

Silk Alley

Leaving the park, we wandered south through the streets of the Jianguomen diplomatic compound. In the States this could have been any wealthy neighborhood—broad, tree-lined streets, minimal traffic, gardeners bent over walled-in flowers. Only the type of protection differed. Instead of watchdogs at the gates, PLA men in sharp green uniforms kept guard.

We passed the corner of the **American Embassy**, its afternoon yard quiet but for the late whir of a cicada. Weekday mornings here buzz with tension. A snaking line of visa applicants forms early, shifting one foot to the next, checking and rechecking papers, talking anxiously in hushed voices. By lunch time the crowd has filed in and dribbled out, emptying the yard for the next day of hopefuls.

Further south is the famous silk market on **Xiushui Street**, also known as "silk alley" or "OK Street," a crushing lane of silk products and other export-quality clothing at low, low prices. We parked our bikes at the end of the street, took a deep breath, and plunged in.

Colors abound—vibrant green and yellow, icy blue, dusky maroon—a feast for the eyes, even if you don't want to buy. It does get a bit exasperating, pushing and being pushed, and there seems to be no rule about when to beat the rush, though weekends are probably best to avoid.

Eastern European buyers make silk alley a regular run. They come with cash, big empty bags, hand calculators, and enough bartering English to get by. They leave with bags stuffed full of silk shirts, scarves, jackets, and lingerie. Jeans and denim products are other popular and profitable commodities for this crew. Mountains of clothes and their owners jostle out of Beijing every Saturday on the eight o'clock Trans-Siberian train, traveling the modern "silk road" to Moscow. If you want something to do on a Saturday night, take in the free show at the Beijing Railway Station; seating in the first-class waiting room is included.

Every newcomer to Beijing loses all common sense in the silk market. "Can you believe how cheap everything is?" "What a great deal!" "I'd better buy a couple of these. They'll make perfect Christmas presents." Jan and Erron were no exception. Waddling through the stalls, our own packs were soon stuffed to bursting like the red-white-and-blue sacks destined for the Russian train.

Rockefeller in Beijing

The afternoon sun full in our faces, we turned back toward the Dongdan intersection. North under the pedestrian overpass and a turn into the second hutong on the left took us past an enclave of traditional Chinese-style buildings. In 1915 John D. Rockefeller poured seven million of his oil dollars into **Peking Union Medical College and Hospital** (Xiehe Hospital, also called Capital Hospital). The two occupy the site of a former prince's mansion. His Foundation continued to support the institution until 1949; to this day Capital Hospital is the most modern and best equipped Chinese-administered institution in Beijing. (There are also, of course, clinics in the embassies and

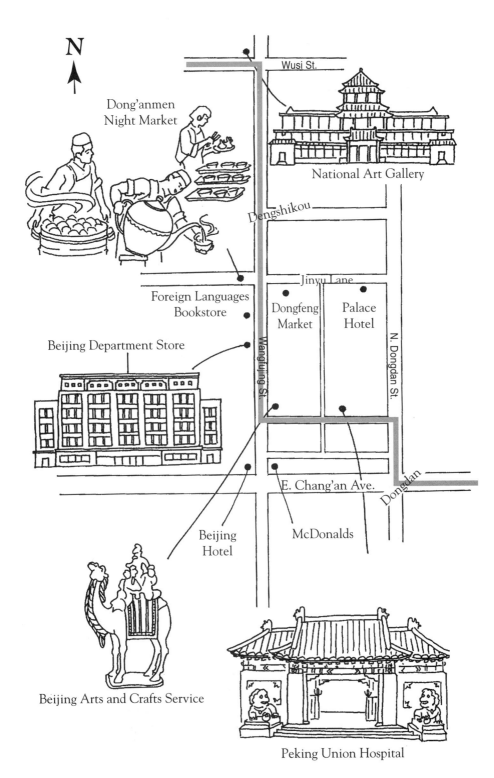

WANGFUJING AREA

the Sino-Japanese Hospital in the northeast corner of the city.)

Both the twenty-four hour emergency service in the ex-prince's mansion near Wangfujing and the new high-rise on Dongdan Street have special sections for foreign residents and tourists. Unless it's after hours or on a Sunday, you should see the doctors in the regular outpatient ward on the sixth floor.

Mansions and a Well—A Short History

Wangfujing, the city's major shopping street, is named for ten princes' mansions built in the Ming Dynasty and their sweet-water well. It was forbidden in those days to dig wells at random near the Imperial Palace. According to the principles of Chinese geomancy, the position of a building or tomb in relation to the natural landscape affects the fortune of its occupants. Drilling into the earth near the emperor's home without allowances for *feng-shui* (wind and water) might have brought ruin to the royal family. The only well in this neighborhood, prized as a scarce commodity, was consequently controlled by the resident aristocracy.

Up until the last few years of the Qing Dynasty, Wangfujing Street was just a narrow dirt alley with a few shops. Around the turn of the century, the developing legation quarter to the south and an expanding number of government offices on the east began to bring in trade. Warlords, new in town after the fall of the last empire, wealthy bureaucrats, politicians, and landlords began to populate the area. Local entrepreneurs saw where the money was to be made and wasted no time in setting up shop—antiques, clocks, furs, and western-style clothes made their debut on

Wangfujing. The street, forever a trend-setter, was paved with asphalt in 1928 to protect the soles of its well-heeled clientele.

Crowd Dodging

Our hutong led us out to the main street at the intersection with the **Arts and Crafts Service**. This three-story spread of gift items offers antiques and knick-knacks ranging in price from dead cheap to barely affordable. On the south side is the **New China Bookstore** (*Xinhua*), Beijing's largest retailer of books. Down across the street is the Beijing Hotel. Bikes are more a hindrance than a help in these busy shopping areas. We parked in the one *mao* lot to free our hands and facilitate crowd dodging.

Sidewalk traffic flow is a problem in all the major shopping districts, but particularly so in Wangfujing, Xidan, and Qianmen, which attract the out-of-town crowds. Don't imagine you can stroll down the packed street, as you might in New York, Hong Kong, or Tokyo. Be ready to stop on a dime, twist to the left, and dodge a flailing arm. No telling what you'll bump into. Wangfujing to the visiting Chinese is an excursion—a tourist must. For out-of-towners unaccustomed to city sights, it can be a baffling adventure requiring sudden stops and starts, backtracks, and sidesteps. When your patience begins to wear thin, remember that some of these folks spend their days tilling the earth—it's not that they're incapable of a straight line.

We wandered along Wangfujing to the **Beijing Department Store**, an unwieldy shopping emporium unfettered by escalators and public rest rooms. The well for which Wangfujing was named is said to have been located in this area. Though recently redone to keep up with the times, this cavernous edifice has seen nearly forty years of recent Chinese history—from the Great Leap Forward through the Cultural Revolution to the last decade of economic reform. It's seen how the needs and interests of generations have changed, and how expectations and incomes have grown.

North a short way brought us to the **Foreign Languages Bookstore**, a state operation dealing in state products and western classics at low prices. Though they rarely have the book you're looking for, they still carry the best selection of foreign language reading material in town. It's also possible, though most don't know about it, to go straight to the source, the **Foreign Languages Bureau** on Baiwanzhuang Road, and buy a book directly from the publisher.

Birds on a Stick

Across the street from the bookstore is the **East Wind Market** (*Dongfeng Shichang*). Originally a parade ground for Manchu troops during the Qing Dynasty, small merchants took over the area in 1903 when they were displaced from their shops two blocks east. It wasn't long before the place bloomed into a mash of stalls, restaurants, and small theaters. The market has since been unified under one roof, and plans are to replace it with one big joint-venture shopping center—yet another to fill the needs of our modern lives with modern products.

Around the corner on Goldfish Alley (*Jinyu Hutong*) is one of Beijing's better known Mongolian hotpot restaurants. **Donglaishun** is an oversized version of the little hotpot diners that line *hutongs* in every neighborhood. Besides the chaffing dish with mutton, they serve dumplings and Peking duck—all Muslim kosher.

Turning west at the intersection, we joined the five-thirty throng in the **Dong'anmen Night Market**. The long trail of food stalls offer deep-fried this and stir-fried that. There are noodles and tiny steamed buns, meat of every calling, and eggs fried in dough. Huge copper kettles of boiling water are tipped to make bowls of thick, sweet almond paste—an acquired taste for those who like to chew their desserts.

Cooks in stained white coats called out as we passed, "Try this, it's delicious!" "Only one *yuan* for a stick. Whaddya say?" Such enthusiasm, often absent from large state-run restaurants, spells out a living based on volume of sales. We passed up the baby quails on a stick and opted for the skewered fish.

Winding Down

Tired after our long day, we doubled back to fetch our bikes and begin the thirty-minute trek home. Judging by the cool strip of blue above the roof line, the sun hadn't much longer to go. Dusty gold leaves whispered as we rode north up Wangfujing Street, past the leather goods, the jewelry stores, the department store, the tea shop, the pharmacy, the snack shop. Wangfujing, south of Goldfish Alley, is officially closed to cyclists during the day (reserved for lurching buses). It opens evenings when rush hour traffic subsides.

One block north of Goldfish Alley is Lantern Market Street (*Dengshikou*). During the Ming and Qing, this was *the* place in Beijing to buy lanterns. Even the women, usually locked up at home, were allowed to come out at night to view the annual gathering of color and light along this street. Transparent ice lanterns made with sprinkled frozen water were once popular, but the art, embodied in the masters' nimble fingers, is now dead. Trade in the market during daylight hours turned to furs and antiques, exotic flowers, and rare plants. There is nothing left today, however, in the cold, tiled surfaces of curb, wall and window to inspire images of those festive, brilliantly lit nights.

West at the next intersection brought us to the **National Art Gallery**, open again after years of renovation. From there it was a straight shot along the northern edge of the Forbidden City to home. We pedaled slowly through the heart of Beijing—past the rippling moat of the imperial residence, past shadowy patches of red and gold on Prospect Hill, past the starry blue North Lake. A light wind sent the trees shivering. Leaves clutched, then fell. Those skipping over the pavement at our wheels would not see the light of day. Pre-dawn sweepers would see to that.

WINTER

The Northern Lakes Area

From Chegongzhuang, east along the Second Ring Road to Yonghegong. To the Confucian Temple, the Drum and Bell Towers in the center of town; around to the Northern Lakes Area and Prospect Park overlooking the Forbidden City.

Preparations

When my dad came to visit last December, we decided to steel ourselves against the weather and tour the northern part of the city by bike. Biking in winter is agreeable as long as there's no heavy wind. Streets are generally clear of the bike mobs encountered the rest of the year, and clear, sunny days abound. The only danger is working up a sweat which, as soon as you get off the bike to do some sightseeing, turns to ice. We dressed in layers and packed another couple sweaters to go. Good gloves (leather or gortex) and wool socks with leather boots (or an equally protective substitute) are a must if you intend to make it a full day.

Our rendezvous point with a couple Chinese friends was the **Lamasery of Harmony and Peace**

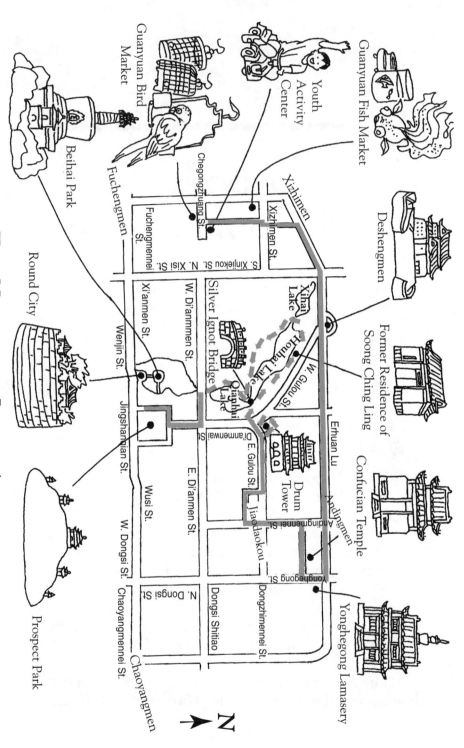

(*Yonghegong*), one of the best known Tibetan Buddhist temples outside of Tibet. It is located in the northeastern corner of the city. We consulted a wall map at home and decided to make a clean shot along the Second Ring Road (*Erhuan Lu*).

The Second Ring Road, mirrored underground by the subway line, is a modern four-lane boulevard that circles the capital in lieu of the now defunct inner-city wall. A handful of renovated city gates are all that remain of the old wall, lending both an aesthetic touch sorely needed on the city's high-rise outer rim and a series of high-visibility landmarks for the bewildered bicyclist.

Old Men's Delight

Well layered and fortified with a couple cups of steaming coffee, we plunged from my over-heated apartment on the west side of town into the freezing morning air. Passing the subway station at **Chegongzhuang**, we ran into the overflow from the neighborhood bird market. Flower, fish, and bird markets are a treat anywhere in China. They pop up in secluded alleyways and great covered emporiums. The one at Chegongzhuang spills from its courtyard into the street with fluffy white kittens and pudgy black puppies nestled in cardboard boxes and bags. Canaries and parakeets and everything cageable swing from low branches and their owner's arms. Nine thirty in the morning, and the market was already hopping.

Never miss the chance to explore these bustling havens of local commerce. We squeezed through the crowd into the market courtyard—to the right, a chorus of chirps, trills and squawks; to the left, stacks of tobacco leaves for the self-roller. Golden hamsters and white mice curled tightly against the cold. There were piles of grain and seed, rows of bamboo cages, and bulging old men in padded army coats waiting for a sale.

In among the bird-cage paraphernalia (porcelain feeders and water dishes) are what the bulging old men insist are "genuine antiques, yes indeed, gen-u-ine antiques. I wouldn't steer you wrong, now, would I?" Raise an amused eyebrow, and they pull out the worn wooden box that holds their special stash. "Now these here are gen-u-ine antiques. I can tell you're a *real* connoisseur." Bargain with a sense of fun and a stiff upper lip. Only gullible foreigners pay the asking price.

Across the street another padded fraternity swarmed and clucked round their birds. The hutong west of the **Youth Activity Center** is lined with more "antique" and "art" stalls. Though prices here may be lower than in other places that cater to foreign shoppers, amused skepticism, even if you don't really mean it, can do no harm.

Pedaling north up the alley, watchful for potholes and pedestrians, we came upon another pet-lover's paradise, the tropical fish market. No more than a long covered walkway, this is where residents of the West City District come for all their fish-related needs. Tanks, pumps, rocks, aquatic plants, and fish. Fish of all shapes, sizes, and colors. Here, indeed, the price is right. Blue tetra for only five *mao*—the price scrawled in black ink on the side of the tank.

Northern Loop

Our hutong led us on to the Second Ring Road. To our left lay **West Gate** (*Xizhimen*), the former north-

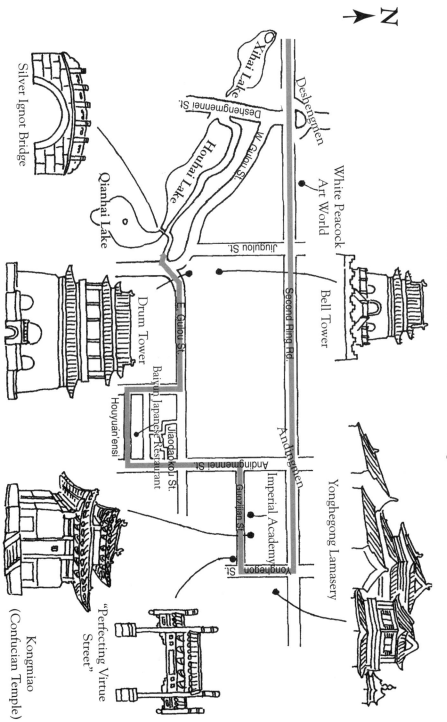

west gate of the Inner City, where camel caravans once plodded in from Mongolia. We turned east along the northern lip that runs the length of the city from Xizhimen to **East Gate** (*Dongzhimen*). Careful not to get over heated, we kept a moderate pace, flowing with the bike lane traffic.

Landmarks along this stretch of road are few. To our left appeared the mountainous **Gate of Moral Victory** (*Deshengmen*), one of the remaining city gates, and across the way, the brightly painted back entrance to the northern lake area (which we were to visit later that day). Then came the **White Peacock Art World**. This colossal six-story wonderland of Chinese arts and crafts is so far from any commercial area, they've got to bring in captive tourists by the busload to generate business.

Coasting down the slight incline at the Andingmen underpass, Dad spotted a padded seat vendor located strategically in bump vicinity. Seat vendor sites are like lemonade stands in the desert. They materialize around the city at respectable intervals, populating underpass and bridge regions where a bicyclist is bound to suffer some nasty jolts. The seats are tie-on foam pads covered with velour for color compatibility. Dad chose red, hoping for good luck, and knotted it securely to the frame.

Pumping up the other side, we passed **Ditan Park**. This place is to the earth as the **Temple of Heaven** (*Tiantan*) is to heaven. The altar (one of eight in Beijing used for sacrifices to natural forces during the Ming and Qing dynasties) was built in the shape of a square—the earth as envisioned in 1530. At Chinese New Year, the annual temple fair fills the grounds with vacationing crowds hot on the trail of snacks, new toys, and colorful, costumed performances.

We turned on Yonghegong Street and followed the red lamasery wall south to the gate. The temperature hovered above freezing, a light breeze stirring the treetops.

State and Church

Shao and Wang showed up in bright down coats and sunny smiles. They'd so eagerly asked about accompanying us, I suspect the prospect of English conversation practice with my father was what pulled them from their warm homes that freezing day. Both were in the computer science program at the Beijing Aeronautical University and former students from my teaching days. They chatted with Dad while I thumbed through my guidebook for information on Tibetan Lamaism. It read:

> Lamaism is a form of Buddhism that contains a large element of Hinduism and popular Tibetan religious worship. "Lama" means "superior one." Buddhism entered Tibet in the eighth century, where it was influenced by native cults, and in the thirteenth, it spread rapidly into Mongolia and north China. Lamaism was especially encouraged by Emperor Qianlong as a means of maintaining political unity within Mongolia and Tibet.

The lamasery has a long and twisted history. Emperor Kangxi of the Qing Dynasty had a mansion built for his son and successor, Prince Yong, on this site in 1694. When the prince became Emperor Yongzheng, his home was declared a Lama temple. According to current statutes, imperial residences could not be reverted to secular use. Fire destroyed the place shortly thereafter, but Yongzheng built it again, naming it

Yonghegong (Palace of Peace and Harmony); using the Yong from his own name. When Yongzheng died in 1735, his son, Emperor Qianlong, ordered the green roof tiles to be changed to the imperial yellow. Then, following his mother's wish, he had it formally converted to a lamasery in 1744, bringing in 500 monks from Mongolia to run the show.

There's a gold vase stored in the temple that also goes back to Qianlong days. In 1792, after quelling disturbances in the far reaches of his empire, Qianlong was determined to get a handle on minority affairs. He commissioned two vases. One is still kept by the Ministry for Tibetan Affairs at Jokhang Temple in Lhasa to determine the reincarnation of the Dalai Lama. The other, in Yonghegong, holds similar powers over the Mongolian Grand Living Buddha. Today, the lamasery is stocked with novices from Inner Mongolia. Prayers are held in the early morning, though the public is not invited.

Temple Chill

Shao stopped to buy a box of Yonghegong brand incense at the lamasery gift shop. They also have a good selection of ink stone rubbings and batik. It's much the same stuff as you can find all over town, but value lies as much in the place of purchase as in the thing itself. And presumably the money goes back to the temple.

Stepping through the second gate, we entered a pleasant courtyard flanked by the drum and bell towers and pavilions housing stele-backed *bixi* (mythological tortoise-like animals carved from stone). Devotees clustered round the bronze incense burner lighting incense for Maitreya (Buddha of the future).

His protectors, the four **Heavenly Kings**, in a hall by the same name, glare woodenly in solid pairs. Veda, in the back, also known as the guardian of Buddhism, gazes serenely into the inner courtyard. The stele pavilion here stands as a tribute to the great cultural melting pot under China's look-alike skin—an essay by Qianlong, inscribed in Tibetan, Mongolian, Manchu, and (Han) Chinese characters, outlines the origins of Lamaism and his own practical reasons for belief (the need to assuage the Mongols).

The next hall, the **Palace of Peace and Harmony** (*Yonghegong*), is where Prince Yong held audience before he ascended the throne. Now the main hall of the temple, it houses the Buddhas of the Past, Present, and Future (Buddhas of the Three Ages) and the eighteen arhats (*lohan*) who were Sakyamuni's disciples.

The **Hall of Eternal Divine Protection** (*Yongyoudian*) was originally Prince Yong's residence. A set of the "eight precious objects" of Buddhism now stand before images of the Amidha Buddha (middle), Tsongkapa (right) and the Buddha of Medicine (left). The **Hall of the Wheel of the Law** (*Falundian*) is the home of Tsongkapa (1357-1419), founder of the Yellow Sect of Lamaism, so called for the yellow robes his adherents wore (still wear) to distinguish them from the older red-robed sects. The throne to the left of his image is reserved for the Dalai Lama, the one to the right for the Panchen Lama. This is where monks gather to study and pray, as we could see by the benches arranged in neat rows. Yak butter lamps burned a low flame; novices paced by the open door clutching strings of beads.

The northern-most hall, the **Pavilion of Ten Thousand Happinesses** (*Wanfuge*) stands backed up against the Yonghegong subway station. Inside is a mammoth Maitreya carved from a single trunk of white sandalwood that was presented to Emperor Qianlong by the Seventh Dalai Lama. A full third of its 26 meters is buried underground to prevent disaster in case of an earthquake.

Turning back the way we'd come, we explored the side galleries that were once used as classrooms for specialized study. On the east is the **Hall of Medicine**, a long, dim room decorated with Tibetan-style *thangkas*. An ancient monk absent-mindedly fingered his beads, bending politely to answer questions of the curious. Across the way, in the **Hall of Mathematics**, we saw where lamas used to work out their astronomy. The courtyard of Qianlong's four-language stele opens to the Esoteric and Exoteric Halls, where multi-armed Bodhisvattas tangled together in myriad poses.

The chill of winter wood and stone has a way of creeping under the skin. We parted gratefully with the darkened rooms and stepped into the eye of light in the first courtyard. Believers buzzed around the bronze burner preparing fistfuls of incense. Clouds of smoke lifted, pillows of white air, past gray and black heads into an ocean of blue. Yonghegong always brings to mind the restless blur of smoky prayers, sweet charcoal scent and powder ash.

Confucian Entertainment

Few, it seems, get around to visiting the **Confucian Temple** (*Kongmiao*). Friends had told me: its nice in the summer, as a quiet getaway from the crowds, but what's the point of a winter visit when the last thing you want is a cool refuge under the trees? But Dad, having recently visited the Kong family temple in Qufu (hometown of Confucius in Shandong Province), couldn't let the chance for further edification pass him by.

The teachings of Confucius (551-479 B.C.) still reach into the social fabric of today. His mark cuts deepest in the management of human affairs, where notions of appropriate behavior dictate the relationship between high and low, powerful and weak. Dividing the world into five cardinal relationships (ruler and subject, parents and children, older and younger brothers, husband and wife, and friend and friend), he taught a code of rites and etiquette aimed at reinforcing the status quo. Imperial worship of the great teacher began in Qufu during the Han Dynasty. Successive generations, intent on maintaining their own status, kept up the practice.

Kublai Khan set up the first Confucian temple in Beijing in the thirteenth century. The present temple, dating from 1306, was rebuilt and refurbished by Empress Dowager Cixi exactly six hundred years later. Though the early years of Communist rule were rough on the great sage—his philosophy was condemned and temples around the country destroyed—he was rectified in the 1980s, having again found approval among the top leadership. Those days of lengthy ritual ceremonies are over. Today the Confucian complex serves as a museum connected to the **Imperial Academy** (*Guozijian*).

The hutong approach to the Confucian temple led us under two decorative archways (*pailou*), a rare sight in modern Beijing. The first reads "Perfecting Virtue Street" and the second, "Guozijian" (the name of the lane, which refers to the Imperial Academy or "school for the sons of state"). Colors in winter are muted, lines sharp. Tree limbs etched charcoal splinters against the cloudless sky. Everything else receded into somber shades of bluish-gray, like a watercolor wash of city rain.

We located the temple entrance about a hundred meters along, across the street from the Confucian Heritage Restaurant. In the first courtyard there is a small forest of 198 steles covered with the names and home towns of 51,624 scholars who passed the triennial imperial examinations during the Yuan, Ming and Qing dynasties. Scattered about in pavilions and cages, they look less like a roll call than a fleet of giant tombstones. The second courtyard extends the graveyard theme: stone tablets that record Qing Dynasty military expeditions.

Approaching the main worship hall, the **Hall of Perfection** (*Dachengdian*), we found ourselves in for a surprise: Yellow robes and pointed Manchu hats met us at the door. No chance of snooping around with costumed musicians on the prowl. We were snatched up and herded in for a performance of Confucian-era music.

The dimpled man who had caught us insisted we listen to his tune tapped out on a series of suspended jade slabs. A stone-age xylophone? Chimes like this were played with bronze bells during important ritual ceremonies throughout the dynasties. Though lacking in color, our musician made up for the melody with his enthusiasm. Every other tap he jerked his head around to beam at us. We beamed back, like anxious parents at a piano recital praying for the end.

At the conclusion of his performance, he wanted to know: Where are you from? What do you do in Beijing? How old are you? How old is your father? Does he like Chinese food? Can he use chopsticks? Our answers were tossed around the costumed group; and pointed hats bobbed cheerfully with every response.

For their next act, a wrinkled old man with sparkling eyes picked up a brown earthenware gourd. Using the blow hole on top and a series of finger holes on the side, he managed to produce a hauntingly sweet melody from the funny little pot. After several encores, he explained that the *tao xun* was adapted from stone whistles used by bird hunters several thousand years ago. His was the new, improved model for modern audio entertainment. Dad let himself be talked into buying a cassette tape of the music for fifteen *yuan,* but he passed up the chance for a xylophone rock priced at only 600 *yuan.*

As for the temple, there are no smiling Buddhas or teeth clenching gods—only memorial tablets for students of Confucius and a single tablet in the center honoring the great teacher. Our friends were reluctant to let us go. They smiled and chatted with us to the door, then directed us around to the back for another unexpected diversion.

There we found a craftsman working vigorously over his stone tablet. An ink blotter the size of a squashed softball in each fist, he pounded with rhythmical precision, bringing to life the image of Confucius on rice paper in black and white. His rubbing complete, he handed Dad the blotters and showed us how to start work on the small student slab he'd prepared to one side. It didn't take long to pick up the rhythm and produce a presentable ink stone rubbing. Our teacher peeled it from the rock and, folding it in two, stuck it in his glass case under the ten *yuan* sign. So that was it—what had appeared a lesson in ink stone rubbing was in fact a plot to exploit the labor of unsuspecting tourists!

Winter Streets

Returning to the hutong, we passed the **Imperial Academy** (*Guozijian*), the highest educational institution in old China. Established in 1306 by the Yuan Dynasty court, it was first a school for Mongol and Chinese boys to study language and martial arts. Upgraded to an institution of higher learning during the Ming Dynasty, the academy taught Confucian classics in preparation for the imperial exams. From the thirteenth to the early twentieth centuries, almost 49,000 candidates studied here. The Academy was most recently renovated in 1956, and now houses the **Capital Library**.

No ticket is required, and as many of the free things in life, this place is one of the best. Come on a late summer afternoon to lean against the lotus balustrade and watch the fishing lines loll in the shadowed pond. Or come in autumn to catch the setting sun glint off the golden roof knob. Or come in winter to peer in the library windows at rows of bundled readers bent eagerly over their books.

Our hutong opened to Andingmennei Street, a busy thoroughfare running from the northern suburbs to downtown. We pedaled past a couple grocery stores, their pyramids of apples, tangerines, and pears stacked beside crates of crimson hawthorn berries—Beijing's winter fruit. Sales clerks—men and women—young and old, resembling the stout bird market vendors, stamped and snorted behind their stacks. I've seen some hearty souls last through the winter without gloves to protect their chapped, reddened hands, but most pull on at least a cotton layer to ease the burning chill.

Traffic ran light. We cruised past the slower cyclists—a mother toting her red bundled two-year-old on a covered seat; a balloon vendor surveying the street for children, his wares dancing colorfully from a bamboo pole; a couple of young fellows hunched over in army great coats, scarves knitted by their girlfriends dangling like limp noodles down their olive green backs. (The length is less a fashion statement than a declaration of love. I have seen some scarves that brush the ground even after several loops around the neck.)

The next intersection leads straight into the **Drum Tower**, a timekeeping relic from the days of old. It towers like a red and green mountain over the plain of gray homes below.

Lunch was next on our agenda. It was time to re-fuel and reheat. We needed not only the calories, but the warmth of a heated room to return feeling to our fingers and toes.

Sushi

South of Jiaodaokou there is a nondescript hutong called Houyuan'ensi running off to the west. There you will find the **Chinese-Japanese Friendship Guesthouse** (*Youhao Bingguan*). Formerly the Yugoslavian embassy, and before that, a Chiang Kaishek stake-out, it's now the headquarters of the **Chinese-Japanese Friendship Association**. Of more likely interest to cold, hungry bike riders, it's also home to the **White Cloud Japanese Restaurant** (*Baiyun Canting*).

The small, unassuming restaurant tucked to one side behind a rockery wall lives up to every recommendation: simple yet tasteful decor, friendly service, delicious food and reasonable prices. It was opened in 1983 as part of the Friendship Association's efforts to promote cultural exchange. Though frequented primarily by Japanese in the early years, it now serves an international crowd.

It was pleasant to leave the cold outside and enter that cozy, softly-lit room, Japanese in every way—from the paper-screen windows and sushi bar to the blue etched bowls and carved toothpicks. My Chinese friends, new to such a place, remarked repeatedly about the aesthetic importance of a meal—as if the idea had never occurred to them before.

Our whole lunch, including sashimi (Shao and Wang didn't appreciate the raw fish nearly as much as the decor) and warm sake for all, came to about 150 *yuan*, high by Chinese standards. But downing my last cup of steaming green tea, I had the impression I'd spent the last hour, not in China, but on a small island to the east. All that was missing was a bow at the door.

Timekeeping Towers

We road on westward. Traffic at the three-way intersection by the Drum Tower seems to increase tenfold; trolley buses, cars, and bikes compete for the narrow street. We slowed to weave into the alley that curves behind the tower, balancing between the mass of carts, bikes, and bodies.

The Drum and Bell Towers were the timekeeping center of the capital for over eight hundred years. Everybody's got a Rolex or Seiko nowadays, but there was a time, not so long ago, when wrist watches were unheard of and clocks a luxury. Londoners had their Big Ben, Beijingers, their Drum and Bell Towers. If you'd lived in the Chinese capital a mere seventy years ago, you'd have known the hour through the night by the drum beat: twice at seven o'clock to "set the watch" with 108 beats and then again at each subsequent two-hour interval until dawn the next day. Had you been an official in the Qing imperial court, you would have begun your day at the third watch (1 am), assembled outside the Meridian Gate at the fourth watch (3 am), and entered the Palace to await royal instructions, kneeling before the Hall of Supreme Harmony, at the fifth watch (5 am). Had you been a gatekeeper posted along the city wall, you would have known to lock up your gate at the first watch and throw it open at the last.

Kublai Khan built Beijing's first Drum Tower, the **Tower of Orderly Administration** (*Qizhenglou*), in 1272. The present model was put up in the Ming Dynasty, when the Imperial Palace was shifted eastward out of the lake area. In 1924, after it had been retired from active service, the Drum Tower took on a new function—the display of artifacts from the 1900 foreign looting of Beijing—and a new name—the **Tower of Realizing Shamefulness** (*Mingchilou*).

We climbed through the brick base to the first landing. There used to be twenty-four ox hide drums upstairs, but only one has survived, its gashed head compliments of the foreign troops let loose in 1900. Also of interest is an explanation of the bronze water clocks that were used to keep time before a major technological breakthrough brought two-hour-incense to the drum tower.

Crime Stoppers

From the northern terrace of the Drum Tower the **Bell Tower** looks like a stern, forbidding fortress, its doors cut like gaping mouths in the gray stone walls. We returned to the street and jostled through the busy market connecting the two former timekeepers. Carts of winter vegetables—cabbage, potatoes, carrots and celery—lined the way. There were stacks of eggs—white, brown, salted, and speckled—and chunks of tofu—salted, spiced, and dried. There were peanuts and oil, grains and seeds. Fish swam circles in their tarp-rigged pools on the back of bicycle carts, mindless of their fate.

We were almost at the Bell Tower when shouts rang out from behind, and the faces around us gleamed with new interest at the action in the street. I looked over to see a woman vendor standing calmly beside her bicycle cart in the eye of the storm. Three plainclothes officials watched a uniformed fourth punctuate rapid-fire speech with angry gestures. The gathering circle bristled with anticipation.

I saw a fellow in the crowd reach inside his long padded army coat to pull out a thick wad of money. Peeling off a ten *yuan* note, he slipped it to the woman when the authorities turned on a second unlicensed offender. She handed it over with a great sigh and was released after one last burst of official indignation. (Though a stall license runs only about 300 *yuan* a month, there aren't enough spots to go around. It's worth the gamble, at ten *yuan* a day, to set up in an unlicensed site and sell produce.)

The chief congratulated his subordinates on a job well done with a round of imported cigarettes. Seeing that the show was over, the onlookers drifted apart, debating like a crowd fresh from the theater the highlights of the scene just witnessed. Vendors returned to their selling, shoppers to their shopping; the crime stoppers sauntered off stage.

The Sound of Shoes

The Bell Tower's earliest predecessor had been a temple. It burned down, as did the next. Emperor Qianlong then made sure this would never happen again. In 1745 he built a solid tower of stone and brick, so solid, in fact, that the only thing shaken loose in the 1976 Tangshan earthquake was a small decoration from the roof.

The original iron bell, cast in 1420, was said to have lacked volume. Usurped by a bronze ringer, it now enjoys a quiet life of semi-retirement in the **Big Bell Temple** (*Dazhongsi*) on the Third Ring Road (Sanhuan Lu). The bronze bell had a range of twenty kilometers, enough to keep it ringing out the watch through to 1924. Its melodious toll was said to turn soft in rainy weather, producing a sound not unlike the word for shoe (*xie*).

There's an old story about the bell: The Ming Dynasty official charged with casting the bronze bell had been at it for over a year, each attempt as unsuccessful as the last. His daughter, worried about the wrath her father would incur, decided she'd move the gods by sacrificing herself in the molten bronze. Her father managed to save only a dainty embroidered shoe, but the casting was a success, and the emperor built a temple in her memory near the foundry. On stormy evenings, when the bell rang with a desolate *xie* sound, mothers would tell their children, "Go to sleep. The Goddess who cast the bell has come to get her slipper back."

The dark stairway around back took us to the upper landing, where, after a perfunctory inspection of the grand old bronze bell, we leaned against the parapet to watch the movement below. Tiny figures moved in circles over the ice on **Qianhai**, one of three connecting lakes north of Beihai Park. The tinkle of bike bells and rhythmical clap of a repairman on his rounds rose above the traffic's hum. Smudges of gray drifted aimlessly over the dark roof tile. Smoke like this covers the city with dust every winter, thanks to the thousands living in courtyard homes who rely on thousands of charcoal briquette stoves to eat and stay warm.

We walked back through the market, quiet after the recent excitement, and mounting our bicycles, headed south from the Drum Tower along **Di'anmen Street**. Di'anmen is a thriving commercial district packed with traffic that flows with a rhythm of its own. Don't try to force it, I told Dad. Just go with the current and look out for rocks.

Concentrated Commerce

A short spurt through the crush landed us at the first hutong on the right. **Yandai Lane** was the commercial center for long-stemmed pipes during the Ming and Qing dynasties. (Look for the historical marker in Chinese and English posted on the wall to the south). For us, it marked the beginning of our jaunt through the **Northern Lakes Area**, a section of town rich in architecture and history.

Wang lived in this neighborhood as a child and knows the streets well. He led us into Yandai Lane, a narrow, no-cars-allowed alley, past matchbox restaurants and crumbling gates. A dignified wooden doorway to the right caught my eye. The public bath, Wang announced; look at everybody with towels around their necks and plastic bags of soap and shampoo on their arms. Most go for the showers rather than the small, dingy tubs. For hutong residents who have

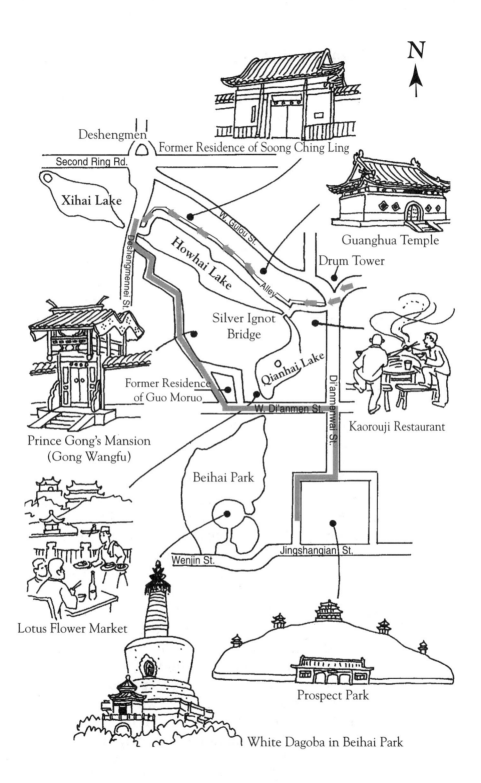

QIANHAI TO PROSPECT PARK

no place to wash at home, it's either that or scrub up in the showers at work.

As we stood there talking, I noticed the three hair salons across the way. Three. Side-by-side. Contrary to contemporary Western business practice, commerce in China is often concentrated around a single theme, reminiscent of the old markets where sellers and buyers met in common interest over a particular product (or line of products). Witness, for example, streets in Beijing bearing the names of the old city markets—Rice Market Lane, Fresh Fish Market Lane, Coal Market Lane, Jewelry Market Lane. Witness also Long-stemmed Pipe Lane, which now might better be called "Hair Salon Alley."

Gazing at Life

A few paces around the corner, the rich smell of frying oil caught our noses. There, in a tiny hovel, not much more than an opening in the wall, stood a two-woman factory. One rolled and cut dough, the other fried and strained chips. The proprietor, a middle-aged man sporting buck teeth, popped his head out for the sale. He carefully weighed our purchase, throwing in an extra handful, nodding and smiling at Dad, who'd stepped up to take the bag. The two carried on an amicable conversation, dad crunching his appreciation while the shopkeeper detailed the cooking process, from the thickness of the dough to the temperature of the oil. Dad nodded, as if all had been made perfectly clear, and pushed off with a confident "*xie-xie*." "He speaks perfect Chinese," the shopkeeper exclaimed to his awed assistants as we wheeled down the lane.

A freshly painted liquor and cigarette shop marks the next corner. We turned left and arrived at **Silver**

Ingot Bridge (*Yingdingqiao,* so named for its resemblance to an ancient form of Chinese currency). This white marble crossing cuts a line between **Front Lake** (*Qianhai*) to the south and **Back Lake** (*Houhai*) to the north. Wang explained that the view from there of the Western Hills, especially at sunset, sunrise, or after snowfall, was considered one of the eight great scenes in old Beijing. So great, in fact, that it inspired a popular saying: "gazing at the hills from the Silver Ingot."

Leaning our bikes against the bridge, we took a moment to look around the lakeside neighborhood. The hutongs there follow no rule. Lined by simple courtyard homes banked up side-by-side, they wind and meet as if by whim. Where traffic ran light, children played children's games—hopping, tapping, throwing, and jumping. Where traffic ran or not, adults played adult games—chatting, dealing, buying, repairing, strolling, and smoking. Everywhere there was life, movement, and noise. I had the feeling as I stood there that if the men were to grow long braids and the women to put on silk trousers, if the mini-vans were transformed into rickshaws, I would be gazing at a fine winter day in the Qing Dynasty.

A row of skeleton willows followed the lake edge, sweeping out of view to our left. Qianhai in summer is a resort for swimmers, boaters, and loungers. When the weather turns warm, the willows blossom into dancing green tails, and the fun seekers glide, not over the water, but under.

North of Qianhai, just around the corner from the bridge, is a 140-year-old eating establishment that used to cater to neighborhood royalty. Manchu princes—the likes of Prince Chun, Prince Gong, and Prince Qing—frequented Kaorouji for roast mutton (similar to Mongolian BBQ), hotpot, and other tasty Muslim-certified dishes. The present building went up in 1927, but the same recipes of yesteryear delight the modern gourmet.

Pulling away from the bridge, we followed Wang around the northern side of Houhai. A group of youngsters scratched vigorously over the ice, hockey sticks and expletives clattering. More courtyard homes edged our way, their lines smoother, fixtures cleaner, doorways wider. Among them is Prince Chun's mansion, birthplace of the Last Emperor Xuantong (Puyi) and his younger brother Pujie. The building is now occupied by the Ministry of Public Health. A couple hundred meters along we came to the solid bright red gate of Soong Ching Ling's former residence.

Life in Pictures

Soong Ching Ling was an extraordinary person. Her long life sparkles with purpose and unwavering direction, as seen in the exhibit of black-and-white photos in the halls of her former home. Our visit to the rooms in which she spent the last years of her life was one of the highlights for us that day.

Once the garden of a Manchu prince's mansion, the grounds have retained their park-like ambiance. A frozen stream, lined with rocks and tilted trees, set the scene. In the exhibition rooms, Soong's life is mapped out in phases, thematically arranged and well-documented—from her early twentieth century student days in the United States and marriage to Sun Yat-sen in 1915 to times of increasing political activism, work with the Communist Party, work for the cause of children, and death in 1981.

I was struck by the abrupt smile that appears on her face in pictures taken after 1949. All the years before, she had posed, stately and stern, beside her husband, with national leaders, with foreign writers and journalists sympathetic to the cause of the Chinese people, lips pressed together seriously. In the second exhibition hall, her smile suddenly lights up, and not just once, but again and again for the rest of her life. It's the kind of smile that can't be faked, the relieved smile of victory after long struggle. The ironic twist to her story is that she was admitted into the Chinese Communist Party and named Honorary Chairwoman of the People's Republic of China just days before her death.

The rooms of her house upstairs are maintained in the same simple, elegant style she kept when she was alive, her favorite books and writing tablets still stacked on the tables for reading. A visit to Soong Qing Ling's former home opens the eye to another level of material comfort in China. The exhibit downstairs provides one more perspective on modern Chinese history. It's open every day but Monday and Wednesday, 9 to 11:30 am and 1:30 to 4:30 pm.

Lake History

Circling around the northern edge of Houhai, we crossed the canal link to **West Lake** (*Xihai*). More commonly known as Jishuitan (Reservoir Pool, "collect-water-pool"), this small park-enclosed body of water is the northern-most of the Northern Lakes.

Centuries ago, Houhai and Jishuitan were part of a busy river port on the teeming waterway connecting outlying rural areas to the heart of the capital. Grain barges were unloaded here in the time of Kublai Khan. An eye-witness report from 1293 has the Great Khan observing "a convoy of boats linked stern to stern, so numerous as to render the water invisible."

By the Ming Dynasty, however, the canals were too silted up for boats to sail that far inland, and the lakes had become a resort area for high officials and nobility. Pleasure boats replaced the grain convoys. Upper-class villas and gardens sprouted along the shores. Though the villas remained, each successive turn of power brought in new owners to enjoy the lakeside life. During the Qing Dynasty, it was the Manchu princes; after the Revolution of 1911, it was the scholarly elite. But without help from the national coffers, the place gradually began to run down, and so now remains, in a state of dignified dilapidation.

What had it been like when boats ran those waters —when low wooden barges, cumbersome with newly harvested wheat, plowed steadily down lake to unload their precious cargo at dock's edge? When wine boats taller than the buildings themselves floated shoreside, filling the air with drunken shouts and shrill laughter? The silent chill of the winter afternoon offered no answers, only circles left by skaters and a chalky outline of sky.

Princely Mansion

Hutongs have a habit of looking the same, which makes the arrival at a desired location sometimes a hit-and-miss affair. We were determined to find **Prince Gong's Mansion** in that weave of untidy lanes. Even Wang, who claimed comprehensive expertise of the area, pulled us down one lane after another in his search for that illusive mansion. Finally, on a deserted hutong, in the arc between Houhai and Qianhai, he spotted the plaque in Chinese hanging on the wall.

Prince's mansions for the royal relatives began to populate the Inner City about five hundred years ago during the Ming Dynasty. They were all designed basically the same. Ceremonial halls and living quarters were lined up south to north facing the sun, just like the Imperial Palace. Though some variation was allowed in the side wings, the central halls had to follow exact specifications, rendering them equal in size throughout the capital.

At Prince Gong's place, only a red and green skeleton of the former grandeur remains. Its nine courtyards, outlined and intersected by covered walkways, make it one of the largest private residential compounds in Beijing. We pushed quickly through, as the chill was gaining an upper hand, wondering what it must have been like to pass the winter there. Paper windows, however intricate the lattice work, do not cut the cold. Exposed to the elements, with only small charcoal stoves, heated beds and layers of silk, even high ranking nobility were not exempt from winter's tribulations. I felt sympathy especially for the women, who, locked up inside, spent their days pushing needles, managing the house, and waiting on the men—none of these particularly heat-generating activities.

The garden, though a lovely jungle of green in the warmer months, was predominated by the only thing left standing in that cold—rocks. Elaborate rockery lines the walkways and builds the garden contours with mini "mountains" and "lakes." Story has it that this particular mansion was the model for Tsao Hsueh-chin's eighteenth century classic, *A Dream of Red Mansions*. It was here that Tsao was supposed to have lived the life of sumptuous decadence he wrote about in his novel (see the *Spring* section for more on this story and a description of the garden replica in the southwest corner of the city).

Lakeside Snacks

The sun was shifting to the west by the time we emerged on the street. Winter days in Beijing are disappointingly short, the light already beginning to fade by 5 pm. We still had time for a bite to eat before sunset, so we looped back around to the **Lotus Flower Market** by Qianhai.

Parking before the wheeled stands, we joined the crowd in search of a snack. A strange, repugnant odor warned us of what lay ahead. There, in sloppy piles, were boiled pig innards—stomachs, kidneys, livers, intestines—ready for slicing into a bowl and garnishing with coriander. The locals take a keen liking to this delicacy, but our gourmet sensibilities overpowered our sense of adventure, and we passed on quickly to the fried cakes and steamed buns.

Around the corner by the lake renovated shops take over where the stands leave off. The tables at lake's edge, packed in summer with ravenous swimmers, courting couples, and families of three, sat quiet but not entirely deserted. A handful of hardy diners slurped their soup in the crisp air, cigarettes burning to the knuckle. We made our selections from the one-pot meals on the outdoor charcoal burner and hastened inside to warm our hands at the stove.

Four little ceramic pots on wooden hot plates arrived with a couple rounds of mini steamed buns. The stewed chicken and barbecued pork were everybody's favorites, the fish and tofu pots a close second. All were too salty, as is often the case with Chinese food—especially that which lacks other distinctive flavors—but palatable when washed down by beer. These one-pot meals are at any rate an interesting alternative to restaurant fare.

We hurried back to the bikes for our last stop—Prospect Hill. To the south lay **Beihai Park**, the old imperial "Winter Palace." Every Chinese who visits Beijing, as evidenced by the crowds, fits Beihai into the tour. But the sun was low, and we still wanted to climb the hill for a view of the Forbidden City. Below is a brief description of Beihai for those who make the time.

The Winter Palace

Beihai thrived as an imperial pleasure ground for most of its thousand years and even ruled for a short spell as the center of the capital. It started in the Liao Dynasty when emperors took to stopping here for the scenery on excursions into the great outback. During the Jin Dynasty, the rulers took enjoyment a step further and built an imperial villa on the spot. They put an artificial hill in the middle of the lake, embellishing it with Lake Taihu stones carted in from the Song Dynasty palace at Bianliang (present-day Kaifeng). The island's name, **Hortensia Isle** (*Qionghua Dao*), hearkens back to this period.

When Kublai Khan broke through the Great Wall and razed the Jin capital in the early thirteenth century, he set up base on the plain and took Beihai as his Imperial Palace. The former Hortensia Isle pleasure palace was thus converted to the Khan's work hall. It so remained, for almost two hundred years, the center of operations in the Chinese capital. The black jade urn displayed in the pavilion inside the **Circular Wall** (*Tuancheng*) is one reminder of those Yuan Dynasty days. Said to have held the Great Khan's wine, it was later found in the hands of some Taoist priests who'd been using it as a pickle barrel.

Emperor Yongle of the Ming Dynasty moved his palace to the east a few paces, retaining Beihai as a pleasure garden. In 1651, under counsel of his Lamaist advisors, Qing Dynasty Emperor Shunzhi had the Hortensia Isle palace replaced with an enormous onion-shaped dagoba for the Tibetan Dalai Lama's upcoming visit. The onion, known as the **White Dagoba**, still rises above a forest of rocks meant to resemble the caves of Taoist Immortals. Lamaist scriptures and other sacred objects are rumored to have been sealed inside the dagoba, but we'd need a fairly big earthquake to shake the truth out of it.

Emperor Qianlong found time in his busy schedule to add several new structures to the island. **The Hall of Beneficent Causation** (*Shanyindian*), built of glazed bricks, has one hundred glazed ceramic images of Buddha set in its walls. A multi-armed Goddess of Mercy (*Guanyin*) juggles her treasures front and center. From the terrace you can see the lakes in Beijing's new "Forbidden City," Central and South Lakes (*Zhongnanhai*), and the walls of the old Forbidden City. Also on the island is the **Pavilion for Inspecting Old Script** (*Yuegulou*), where 495 samples of work by famous calligraphers carved in stone during Qianlong's day have been preserved.

Qianlong, like Han Dynasty Emperor Wu Di, had a fascination with longevity, as the Bronze Immortal on the northwest slope of the island testifies. Wu Di believed that if he drank dew from Heaven collected in a bronze bowl he'd live eight hundred years. In 104 B.C. Wu Di had an image of an immortal holding a bowl cast in bronze and placed in a palace outside his capital at Chang'an (now Xi'an). Some fifteen centuries later, Qianlong ordered images of bronze immortals placed around Beijing, ensuring himself a constant supply of the life-prolonging dew. Though the result was several hundred years shy of the eight hundred mark, Qianlong did manage to get in a good sixty-year reign.

Another point of interest on the island is **Fangshan**, a classy restaurant that serves Empress Dowager Cixi dishes at imperial prices. The recipe for their sesame seed biscuits stuffed with minced pork is said to have come to Cixi one night in a dream. For those who wish to cross the lake, there are ferries that leave from the nearby boat dock or rowboats for rent along the northern shore. In winter, it's even easier: muffle up and walk across.

On the north side of the lake you will find a second little pleasure haven. The **Five Dragons Pavilion** (*Wulongting*), built in 1651, was a favorite get-away for emperors who came to fish and gaze at the moon. The **Iron Screen** (*Tieyingbi*), so called for its iron-like finish, and the **Nine Dragon Screen** (*Jiulongbi*), made of colored glazed tiles during the Ming Dynasty, still stand to scare off evil spirits. The **Hall of Heavenly Kings** (*Tianwangdian*) has entered the modern age as a revamped Youth Science and Technology Hall.

Beihai hasn't changed much since Qianlong's day. Opened to the public in 1915, it has for decades remained a favorite weekend destination. Warm summer nights bring the strollers; fall and spring attract season watchers; winter afternoons fill up with skaters. If Qianlong's dew-drinking trick had worked, he'd still be around to watch the crowds on ice, just as he used to review imperial skating parties in the late 1700s.

Sunset View

Back to our story. We had to hurry down Di'anmen Street to **Prospect Hill** (*Jingshan*) before daylight faded into dusk. Entering from the western gate, we ran up the path to the pavilion at the top.

Chilly as it was, a small crowd had gathered under the curving eaves and along the rockery below to enjoy the last rays of dusty gold over the russet roofs of the Forbidden City. In pre-skyscraper days, **Prospect Hill**, also known as Coal Hill (*Meishan*) for the coal stored below, was the highest point in the Inner City and the best place to look out over the capital. It's still a great choice for a view of the city.

Like every major park in Beijing, Prospect Hill was a forbidden garden to all but royalty and their retinue for most of its long history. The hill was "built" under Kublai Khan's direction with earth dredged from the Imperial Palace moat and nearby lakes, then stocked with small wild animals to produce a rural feel. So it's actually the dump heap of a massive Yuan Dynasty lake excavation project. Each of its five peaks is topped with a pavilion, courtesy of Qianlong, which at one time housed five bronze Buddhas. Only the one atop the highest peak remains, the rest having been snatched away by the Western troops in 1900.

On the east side of the hill there was once a locust tree used by an emperor to hang himself. As the tale goes, the last ruler of the Ming Dynasty, Chongzheng, ran out of the palace on the morning of March 19, 1644—crownless, hair flying, long white dragon-embroidered gown flapping—having just learned that his troops had surrendered to a peasant army. He raced panic-stricken to the top of Prospect Hill, one shoe lost along the way, denounced his subordinates for having forsaken him (he'd just killed his concubine and two princesses), and walked down to hang himself by his belt. A wooden plaque marks the unfortunate spot.

From the top, we could see Beihai to the west, scattered still with skaters. To the north lay the lakes we'd just visited. Overhead lights around Qianhai's night rink glowed palely in the bluish pre-dusk sky. Row after row of courtyard homes beamed up at us with the bustle of dinner preparation. In the distance stood the capital's retired timekeepers, silent now through the night.

Quiet in winter is unlike quiet in any other season. For a moment the sun balanced, a half dish on the horizon, and nothing moved. Then, as if remembering, it sank behind the ragged edge of purple hills, and the city bumped back to life. I could hear the squeeze of cars and buses on the street below, the blaring horns and soft clatter of voices. We descended the hill, said our good-byes, and rode home in the gathering dark.

SPRING

The Old Chinese City

From Baiyun Temple in the southwest along the canal to the Grand View Garden; north through Ox Street to the Xuanwumen District and Liulichang. South along Qianmen Street to the Temple of Heaven in the Tianqiao District, looping back through Qianmen.

Waiting out the Winds

y colleague Shou and I talked all winter about going to explore the southern reaches of the capital. We'd been to the **Temple of Heaven** (*Tiantan*) and the shopping districts around Qianmen, but that maze of alleys and markets that made up what was once known as the "Chinese City" remained a mystery to us.

For centuries the "Chinese City" had been a rambling shanty town clinging to the edge of the fortified Inner City (the area within the Second Ring Road). During the Ming Dynasty, it was officially incorporated into the capital as the Outer City. When the Manchus conquered Beijing in 1644, they banished the Han Chinese to this southern district. In no time,

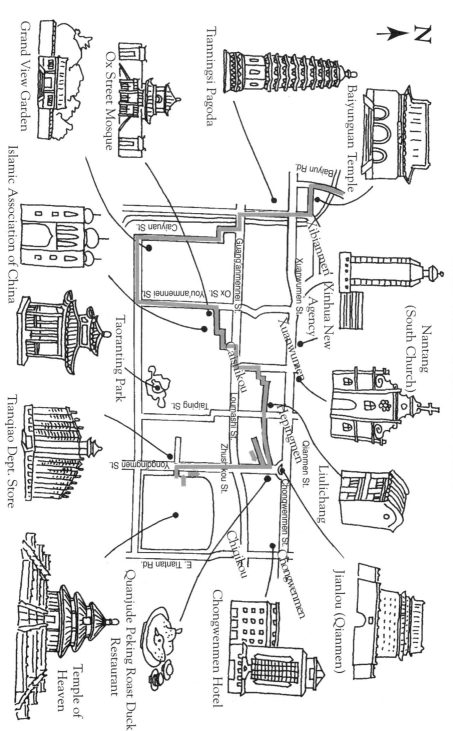

the area around Qianmen Street blossomed into the capital's business and entertainment hub—where deals were made and nobility played. Local flavor. Local history. We waited for a break in the weather to spend a day in search of Old Beijing.

Early spring brought the usual tremendous winds, coating the capital with a layer of grit from the Gobi Desert. A quick walk to the neighborhood store at this time of year requires protective eye, nose, and mouth gear. Cotton surgical masks and translucent scarves are put to good use. Women and little children take on the look of colorful mummies with their faces wrapped up in layers, while manly men and unsuspecting tourists endure the full brunt of the wind in stinging lashes across the face. The days of dusty orange light, when the sun is cloaked in a screen of flying sand, come rarely enough to be appreciated as infrequent guests who add interest to the season. Some years they overstay their welcome.

By late April the sky had cleared to empty blue, blotted only occasionally by a distant pale haze. Potted flowers appeared on the sidewalks and windowsills. Leafing poplar released its clouds of floating white cotton. Gone were the mummies and the surgical masks, back were the bikes and the sun. Shorts and T-shirts reappeared in the markets and, to the perpetual amazement of the Chinese, on the bodies of foreign residents and tourists. (Indoctrinated in the principles of traditional Chinese medicine, most Chinese are well padded the year through. My colleagues wear long johns every day from October to April.)

We planned to make a snaking tour through the large canal-enclosed rectangle, beginning in the northwest corner by **West Access Gate** (*Xibianmen*), looping our way past parks and through various market streets, and winding up at the Temple of Heaven.

Buses run all the major routes in that area, and walking is always an option. But nothing's better than a bike for flexibility and freedom.

Daoist Monastery

The last Saturday in April dawned sunny and clear. We suppressed the urge to leave work and waited until the next morning to set off on our adventure, Shou in her jeans and I in my shorts. Our first destination was the **White Cloud Temple** (*Baiyunguan*), the largest Daoist complex in Beijing and headquarters for the Dragon Gate Sect. Approaching from the north along Baiyun Road, we spotted the slanting temple roofs among the squared-off, hatless buildings of a less-inspired era. There's no obvious entrance from the road; left down a winding hutong brought us to the main gate, protected in front by a red wall that reads in big gold characters "Everlasting Spring."

The architecture at Baiyunguan is Qing Dynasty: multiple courtyards set on a central north-south axis, curving eaves, red lacquered wood doors, and windows. The Daoist priests are also Qing Dynasty: long hair looped up in topknots, short blue robes, white leggings, and black cloth shoes. Wandering about, we felt like we were on a movie set for a kung-fu flick. But the Shaolin monks, rather than breaking out in a frenzy of chops and kicks, were leading small groups around the temple, modestly answering questions and explaining Daoist philosophy.

A bridge in the second courtyard offers some entertainment value and, if your aim is good, eternal luck. We bought a handful of small copper disks for one *mao* each and hurled them at the bell hanging below, like you do at the county-fair coin toss. The difference is, at a fair, if you peg a green glass ashtray, you walk away with a green glass ashtray. At Baiyunguan, if you ring the bell, you walk away with luck to last a lifetime. Fortunately there's no penalty for missing.

Baiyunguan has been the center of Daoism in northern China for about seven hundred years. When Qiu Chuji, a priest from Shandong Province, was appointed by Kublai Khan as the "National Teacher" in charge of all Daoist affairs, he made his headquarters here. Hall after hall display the golden kings and emperors of the Daoist pantheon. An image of Qiu himself occupies a prominent position in the center of the last courtyard.

The side galleries, on closer inspection, reveal a range of unusually animated gods. Though the buildings are laid out much the same as those of the Buddhist faith, the deities take on a completely different look—less meditative, more Chinese. *Lingzhi* mushroom and cranes (both symbols of longevity), Daoist immortals, and the Eight Diagrams replace the Buddhist lotus, Bodhisvattas, and scriptures imported from India.

Prayer services are open to the public on holidays. The biggest event here is the temple fair at Chinese New Year, which draws record-size crowds. To the Chinese, noise and excitement indicate prosperity and happiness. Baiyunguan, a peaceful haven most of the time, grows unbearably rich with festivities the first week of the lunar new year. Like many places in town, the temple is closed to visitors on Monday.

Industrial Moat

Leaving the temple, we wound our way out of that small, cluttered neighborhood until we located the bike lane leading south next to a newly built Second Ring Road on-ramp. The whole area is a mass of construction sites in (or, as the case may be, out of) process. There are few endearing qualities. Stark twenty-story apartment buildings rise through the factory-smudged air; cars race by on the "expressway." Though there are plenty of bridges over to the Chinese City, they are mostly flat fingers of concrete. The moat is now a tiled, wide mouth channel of shallow brown water, thick with industrial run-off. Trees, grass, and signs of life other than the bodies hurrying by, are few. It's the very picture of metropolitan sprawl conjured up in a once futuristic, now historical, novel.

The thirteen-story stone pagoda that rises out of the concrete and steel junk yard is the oldest building in Beijing. Built as part of the **Temple of Heavenly Peace** (*Tianningsi*) during the Liao Dynasty about a thousand years ago, it occupied prime real estate in the most flourishing market district of the imperial city. The temple and market are gone. The pagoda stands webbed in by construction scaffolding, apparently with big plans for a twentieth century face-lift. As some things are better appreciated from afar, we didn't attempt to pick our way in for a closer look.

We crossed a concrete finger to the Chinese City and turned south along the road by the moat, pumping hard against the headwind. Spring wind usually blows in from the north, but buildings have a way of bending air to create new paths of flow. Tired of the beating at our faces, we ducked into a brick-lined hutong where a wheeled *Tianjin Bing* stand waited against the wall. (Tianjin, a city 140 kilometers to the southeast of Beijing, is said to be the birthplace of a unique pancake, or *bing*, fried on flat slabs in covered carts.) At only one *yuan* each, we knew we were in a cheap part of town. These rolled crepe-like snacks with fried egg, green onion, and sauce usually go for at least half again as much.

I watched the neighborhood kids while Shou waited for her *bing*. Pairs of junior high school girls, attached at the shoulder, filtered in and out of the corner shop—in with a pocket of money, out with an ice cream bar or bag of candy or yoghurt. Toddlers, still bundled against the cold, waddled at the end of grandma's arm. A little girl, no more than five years old, came charging out of the store alone, vinegar bottle clasped firmly in hand. Shooting a glance across the lane, she darted, in shoes two sizes too big and thick cotton trousers, through a clear spot in the bicycle traffic. Safely across, she slowed her pace to drag the bottle by its neck, bumping all the way home.

Re-living a Chinese Classic

A friend had recommended we visit the **Grand View Garden** (*Daguanyuan*) in the far southwest corner of the Outer City. Buying my ticket was a battle. I couldn't convince the ticket sellers, even with all proper the I.D. cards and documents, that I'm entitled to normal Chinese price (foreigners pay inflated rates for tourist spots, train and airplane tickets, and state-run hotels, unless they work for the Chinese or are students at a Chinese university). In the end, after much discussion and investigation of all pertinent proof, they allowed me to pay in RMB (Chinese money) instead of FEC (foreign exchange certificates), but still at the foreigner price. Scenes like this are typical in over-regulated China, where power of interpretation lies with the individual. Another day, another ticket seller, another outcome.

National Day festivities—Tian'anmen Gate

Autumn

Chestnuts roasting on an open fire

Stocking up for winter

Faces

Spring Festival treats

Winter

The Summer Palace in white

A cool dip

Family transport

Incense for the gods—
Baiyunguan

Spring fashion

Cook

Night Market delicacies

Diamond Throne Pagoda at Wutasi

Summer

Shirt sleeve days

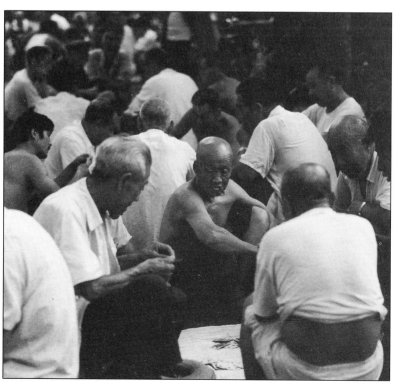

Seeking a cool breeze

Lakeside refreshment

The Grand View Garden was built a few years ago as the set for a TV series based on the Chinese classic *A Dream of Red Mansions*. Written by Tsao Hsueh-chin (1715-1763), this glorified story of unconsummated love in the sumptuous home of a high Qing official is still a favorite of old and young alike.

The garden in the book comes into being when the hero's older sister, who's been married to the emperor as one of his lesser wives, is granted home leave. For an imperial concubine, to return home was no ordinary affair. She had to be provided with the finest of everything and treated with the respect due a member of the emperor's harem. (Her own father, being a man, could no longer look upon his daughter's face, and was required to speak to her through a screen.) Her family broke the bank to build a beautiful garden to welcome her home, a garden that essentially became the private playground of her sisters, girl relatives, handmaids, and pampered little brother, the hero Jia Baoyu.

The exhibits and separate living quarters for each of the characters in the novel don't mean a lot unless you know the story, but the garden is a good example of classical Chinese landscape sculpture. Overall there's a particular flatness distinguished by too much concrete and too little wood. A mockup Qing Dynasty setting shouldn't feel so perfectly new, so unused. Give it a century or two to wear in perhaps.

Working-class Neighborhood

We returned to moat's edge and followed the east-west stretch past more factories and dull brick dormitories. The **Number Two Hospital for Infectious Diseases** lies beyond the water, banned from the city as

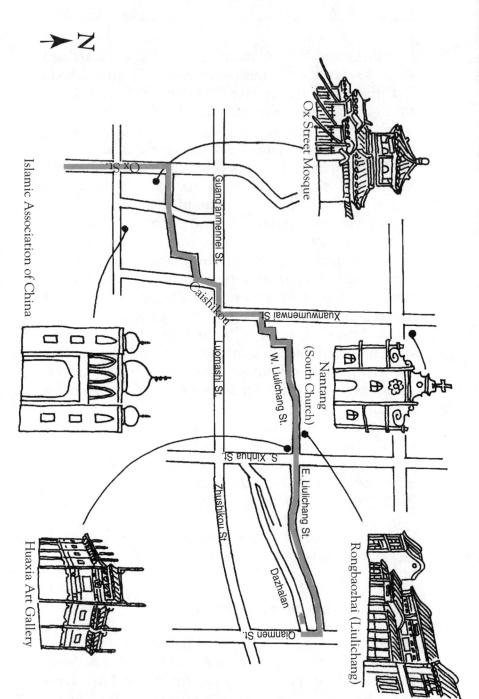

OX STREET TO LIULICHANG

were the Han Chinese during the Manchu era from residential quarters up north. There's a model prison in that quarter where inmates grind out shoes and socks for a Beijing clothing company. Tours around its sparkling halls and clean-swept drives may be arranged through a Chinese contact.

Turning north at the first opportunity took us past more brick—brick apartment buildings, brick stores, brick walls, brick factories. Small sundry shops filled the crevices; a blue-collar crew strolled the sidewalks. There are no palaces or parks here, no broad tree-lined avenues or flower displays, no fancy shops or fancy people. It's a Bruce Springsteen kind of neighborhood, the New Jersey of Beijing.

Further on, the scene shifts back to the familiar gray of Beijing's traditional courtyard housing. Ox Street (*Niu Jie*), in the Guanganmen area, is a pleasant reminder of the pre-factory era. Only a few hundred meters long, this Muslim enclave boasts the largest and oldest of more than eighty mosques in Beijing.

Ox Street Mosque

Shou and I pulled in by the brightly painted gate set at an angle against the street. Muslims must face Mecca when they pray. That explains what appears to be a slip of the architect's rule in the mosque's orientation. The original tenth century Arabic-style building on this site was the work of Nasruddin, the son of a priest who came to preach the Islamic faith during the Northern Song Dynasty. Reconstruction and renovation during the Qing Dynasty and after 1949 have made it what it is today, a mosque with Chinese characteristics. The prayer halls facing Mecca are roofed with glazed tiles; red roof arches and posts are inscribed with texts from the Koran.

The alley on the right led us past the pre-prayer ablution bathhouse, where worshipers must wash themselves in key locations before entering the mosque. Just through the side gate is the main prayer hall for men, distinguished by the patchwork of prayer rugs arranged over its green carpeted expanse. Shoes and women are not allowed. The Koran forbids portrayal of human or animal images in areas of worship; decoration on the walls is restricted to Arabic script and geometric patterns.

Behind us, to the rear of the complex, was the minaret, where the muezzin goes five times a day to call in the faithful for their prayers. Up by the front gate was the hexagonal **Moon Observation Tower** (*Wangyuelou*), where the Imam goes at the beginning and end of Ramadan (the month of fasting observed by all Muslims) to determine the length of the fast based on the moon's waxing and waning.

In the back of the courtyard, behind the storerooms and down a tiny alley, we came upon the separate prayer hall for women. A mere side room, the women's hall is distinguished by its narrow concrete floor and bare walls.

Of Markets and *Hutongs*

Aside from the mosque, Ox Street offers a good look into one of the minority communities of Beijing. The neighborhood is populated primarily by the Hui people (descendants of mixed marriages between Middle Easterners and Han Chinese from as far back as the Yuan Dynasty). The Hui run their own schools and a hospital here, ensuring the standards of ritual and cleanliness dictated by the Koran for their children and infirm. Restaurants, painted blue and green, are *Qingzhen* (Muslim "kosher"), meaning they have nothing to do with pork or other filthy edibles regularly consumed by the Hans. Qingzhen restaurants can be identified all over Beijing by the squiggly Arabic script over their doors.

East under an arched gateway landed us in the Ox Street farmer's market. Mutton dominated the scene. Piles of lamb—whole legs down to the hoof, shoulders and stomachs, liver, tongue, and ribs—lay exposed to the air on carts and tarpaulins thrown on the ground. The lane reeked of fresh lamb's blood. We hurried on to the fruit stalls and open space beyond.

There a loose crowd had gathered around two stool sitters busily engaged in wash basin repair. A middle-aged man and his daughter crouched intently over their work, tapping, patching, and smoothing rough edges. We joined the circle, all eyes riveted on the work in process. Business was slower for the aluminum pot repairman across the lane. His hammers lay idle beside a couple of old gnarled kettles on a plastic tarp in the shade.

Back on our bikes, we followed the hutong where it would take us, in no rush to find the main road. Slender girls skipped over stretched circles of elastic, soft-soled shoes lightly tapping the asphalt, pony-tailed hair bouncing to the beat. Hula-hoops, the newest fad to hit Beijing, spun around young waists—spun, wobbled, and clattered to the ground. Bicycles, jugs, and barrels competed for a bit of earthen wall on which to lean. Spring weeds tried out their footing between cracks on the peaked-tile roofs above. Here was the old "Chinese City" we'd been looking for—the tone of an ageless pulse, bouncing off dusty shutters, telling tales of fortune and decay.

Unfortunately hutongs must come to an end. Too soon, we found ourselves on the rushing, honking thoroughfare by **Caishikou**. *Caishi* means vegetable market. In the old days, Caishikou was the vegetable hub of the capital. During the Ming and Qing dynasties, the tax on goods brought through the gates into the Inner City created a long commercial strip outside the city wall. East of Caishikou was the Mule and Horse Market (*Luomashi*); beyond that, the Pearl Market (*Zhushi*) and Porcelain Ware Mart (*Ciqishi*). Rice Market Lane (*Mishi Hutong*) cuts south toward Taoranting Park. The markets have long folded into obscurity, but the names remain as signposts of the past.

First Church

The red light at the three-way intersection by Caishikou meant nothing to our east-bound companions. Cars and bikes flowed staunchly past the traffic cop who, by all indication, concurred with their interpretation of the law. At a break in the line of cars, we seized the chance to dart across to Xuanwumen Street.

Back in the days of the city wall, the Front Gate (*Qianmen*) was flanked by the **Gate of Proclaimed Military Prowess** (*Xuanwumen*) on the west and the **Gate of Exalted Civilization** (*Chongwenmen*) on the east. Convicts were led through Xuanwumen on their way to execution, hence its other, less fortunate name, the "Gate of Death." Real estate values in this tainted neighborhood have always been the lowest in town.

In 1605, the Jesuit missionary Matteo Ricci purchased the only land available to him as a foreigner—a plot no Chinese would touch with a ten-foot pole—the one right next to the "Gate of Death." There he built his home and the first Catholic chapel in Beijing. It was enlarged in 1650 under the direction of another Jesuit, Adam Schall von Bell (whose home on Wangfujing also became the site of a Catholic church). Over the next 250 years, it was destroyed and rebuilt three times.

The present cathedral, **South Church** (*Nantang*), was built in 1904, "renovated" by the Red Guards during the Cultural Revolution, and reopened in 1979. It's now one of the main official Catholic churches in Beijing and seat of the Patriotic Society of Chinese Catholics.

Our tour did not take us that far north. We veered off the main road to puzzle our way through the *hutongs* leading to the western end of Liulichang Street. A bent old man in a blue Mao suit pointed us on through the sea of jumbled courtyard dwellings to the edge of the gray brick commercial range.

Glazed Tile and Good Books

The name **Glazed Tile Factory** (*Liulichang*) comes from the old kiln, built here during the Yuan Dynasty. It once supplied most of the glazed ornamentation and tile work for Ming Dynasty halls and palaces. During the Qing Dynasty, Chinese officials who served in the Manchu court but were not allowed to live in the Inner City came to populate the area. Guest-houses for imperial exam candidates and others visiting the capital on business were set up here by provincial and prefectural benevolent associations.

Over time, Liulichang came to be known for its bookstores and antique shops, which grew up around this class of intellectuals—scholars, painters, and calligraphers. With over thirty bookshops, it was a regular haunt of the educated elite in the capital for more than five hundred years. Li Wenzao, a scholar in the Qianlong period of the Qing Dynasty, described eighteenth century Liulichang as such:

> To the south of the kiln is a bridge that separates the tile works into two sections. To the east of the bridge, the street is narrow and, for the most part, the shops there sell spectacles, metal flues for household use, and various daily necessities. To the west of the bridge, the road is wider, and besides the regular bookshops, there are shops selling antiques and other curios, shops specializing in calligraphy books, scroll mounters, professional scribes, engravers of name seals, and wooden blocks for painting, as well as shops where stone tablets are inscribed. Here also are shops offering the articles needed by a scholar participating in the imperial examinations—brushes, paper, ink bottles, paperweights.

Though the tile works is long gone, its plot taken over by a couple schools and a telephone company, both east and west are now a conglomeration of state and privately-run art, antique, and book shops. Government restoration, unfortunately, has transformed Liulichang into something not unlike a tidy Qing Dynasty movie set. The substantial gray brick and red lacquer buildings cut a sterile row against the seething city edge.

Our first stop was the **Commercial Press Bookstore**, a small retail outlet on the north side of the street that carries books in English and Chinese, dictionaries and language textbooks. Shou's brother had asked her to pick up one of those versatile pocket Chinese-English, English-Chinese dictionaries for his upcoming trip to the States.

The air inside was unusually warm. A few customers lingered thoughtfully, drawing books from the shelves, flicking the pages, shifting their weight from side to side. Shou spotted the little red dictionary behind the counter and asked to see a selection (much of the merchandise in China must be inspected for flaws; with books, check for printing quality and creased pages). The saleswoman, in a rare display of good will, pulled out the entire lot to let her choose.

Next door, we ducked into one of Beijing's best known purveyors of traditional Chinese paintings and calligraphy. **Rongbaozhai** (meaning "an honorable name is a priceless jewel") is also known for its colored woodblock reproductions of paintings. Improving upon woodblock printing techniques first developed during the Tang Dynasty, Rongbaozhai artisans have reproduced pictures in such detail, they claim even the artist of the original can't tell the difference!

The scent of ink in the downstairs gallery flooded our senses like a warm spring day in a calligrapher's studio. We paused before the shining glass cases of brushes, ink rubbing stones, rice paper, and stone chops to breathe in the rich blackness. Upstairs, we inspected the unfurled scrolls. Though many of the antiques and works of art to be had in this quarter were bought up by museums in the fifties, some older pieces are still to be found. A chop mark distinguishes the paintings that are "national treasures" not allowed to be taken out of the country.

Eastern Liulichang

On the busy cross street that slices Liulichang in two, we joined the group edging through traffic to the other side. There are a couple secrets to such precarious, far too common crossings: Make sure you're well padded by fellow crossers and leave your fear behind on the sidewalk. At a break in the first lane, march boldly to the center dividing line, bike in tow, and wait fearlessly while cars and trucks stream by, fore and aft, until a hole appears in the second lane. Dash across, and your mission is complete.

Shops on the east side carry mostly antiques and antique-like items at inflated prices. The **China Bookstore**, located in the back courtyard of the first complex on the north, sells used foreign language books. Locking our bikes beside the row of waiting taxis, we passed through a maze of craft and curio stalls. Out the back door to the right we found the glassy half-circle entry we were looking for.

A used bookstore in China, particularly one that deals in English, is a rare pleasure, regardless of its curious organizational style. All the foreign languages are dashed together against one wall. English stands shoulder-to-shoulder with Russian, Japanese, and German. Literature shares shelf space with psychology and history. We thumbed through some of the turn-of-the-century hardbacks stamped with university library and church seals. Antiques like that, worth a fair amount anywhere, go for no small sum in Liulichang. Good deals may be found among the Chinese books, however, if you're patient and know what you want.

The crowded antique shops at the eastern end of the lane are private versions of the roomy government stores in the middle. I poked my head in a doorway to see the "antiques"—glass vials, carved beads, translucent ceramics, mini-Buddhas, and copper coins. Merchants invariably perk up when they see a foreign face, and race to the door with a welcoming "Hello, hello." One prejudice about Western shoppers is that we are big spenders and big suckers. Unfortunately, the gushing sales tactic often works contrary to their best inten-

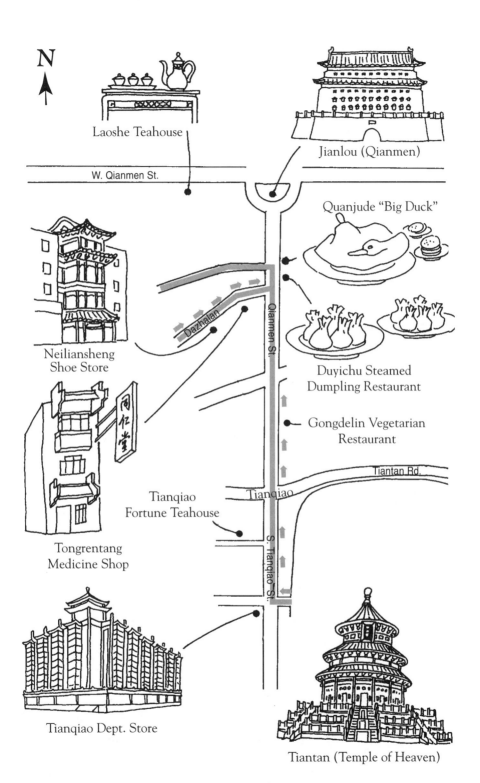

QIANMEN STREET

tions. Put off by the deluge, I dragged Shou away and escaped down the street.

Lunch was next on our agenda. We rode through the hutongs leading to Qianmen Street, balancing past carts of tofu, clothing stalls, and bag-laden shoppers. Mongolian hot-pot restaurants crowded with ruddy-faced men leaning over copper braziers and platters of razor thin mutton lined the way. Zealous shopkeepers called out as we passed, beckoning us in for lunch. But hot pot is a group affair, and we were headed elsewhere.

The Only Place for a Bite to Eat

Duyichu is known in the capital for one propitious winter's night two centuries ago when the Qing Emperor Qianlong rode up Qianmen Street after a long day on the road, hungry and looking for a bite to eat. Du-yi-chu, literally "the one and only spot," was the sole eatery open at that late hour. So pleased was he with their steamed dumplings and fine service, that the emperor picked up his brush upon return to the royal study and penned three characters to present to the shop owner. The name "Duyichu" has stuck. The plaque in Qianlong's hand still hangs on the back wall.

We were greeted inside with the gay chatter and commotion of a six-day-working-week people out on their Sunday binge. Successful dining in China is, on the whole, a very different matter than in the West. Whereas we prize a subdued setting conducive to conversation and intimacies, the Chinese go for *real* atmosphere, the kind that forces everyone to shout across the table to be heard. Duyichu lived up to the requisite for local flavor that day, its packed rooms bursting to the rafters with hot air.

There's no room for polite pleasantries when it comes to seating at a Chinese diner. We pounced on the first chairs available and squeezed in with two other groups already eating around the large round table. Don't expect a quiet table for two in these popular establishments. Unless business is slow, which it almost never is, you'll be sharing space with anyone from a traveling salesman to an actress, from a junior high teacher to a screaming infant.

Qianlong would have certainly been disappointed with the service (not unusual for most large state-run enterprises) but probably pleasantly surprised by the range of delicious Shaomai to choose from. Shaomai are fat little steamed dumplings stuffed with meat and vegetables. We ordered their five-flavor variety pack: crab meat, spinach, mushroom and bamboo, pork, and sweet red bean. They came stacked in bamboo racks, ready for dipping into black vinegar or soy sauce and popping in the mouth. We had a good dozen each, washed them down with egg soup, and walked away with two full doggy bags for a total of twenty-six *yuan*.

Dazhalan

Another favorite eating establishment in that neighborhood is the **Quanjude Peking Roast Duck Restaurant**, better known as the "Big Duck." Inspiration for a popular play describing social change around the turn of the Qing Dynasty, Quanjude has been in business since 1864. Though branches of the same restaurant have taken over in Wangfujing and Hepingmen, Qianmen boasts the original site and the original recipe.

We left our bikes in the lot to explore the **Dazhalan Market,** the swarming hutong of specialty shops, theaters, and department stores we had studiously avoided on our beeline to lunch. Like the market streets to the south, Dazhalan's commercial history began during the Ming Dynasty. Unlike those former trading centers, Dazhalan (literally "big stockades"), or Dashalar in the Beijing dialect, served a dual purpose in those times. By day, it was a busy market; by night, one of some 1,200 sites in the capital where barriers were set up to enforce the nighttime curfew. The street was reduced to a rubble heap when Western powers flexed their muscles in 1900. The present-day structures are all twentieth century.

Passing through the metal gateway off Qianmen Street, we joined the crush of Sunday shoppers and sightseers elbowing through the narrow lane. What a contrast to the stark tidiness of Liulichang just a stone's throw away! Both hold a kernel of old Beijing in their peaked roofs and wood trim, but where the antique street reclines placidly in fresh paint and newly hewn brick, Dazhalan bristles with the passing seasons and tide of human change. Blonde mannequins pose suggestively in polyester sweat suits. Rock music blares. Don't let the interesting architecture fool you—it's the same merchandise to be found in stalls popping up street-side all over the city.

Nonetheless, you'll find some of the oldest shops in Beijing along this hundred meters of crowded hutong. **Liubiju**, with more than four hundred years of history, is still going strong as the definitive pickle and sauce outlet in this corner of the world. **Riufuxiang**, several doors down, has a century under its belt of dealing in fine fabrics—silks, wools, and furs.

Turning right on the first north-south hutong off Qianmen Street will bring you to the **Lao She Teahouse** (*Lao She Chaguan*; named after the Beijing author of *Rickshaw Boy* who committed suicide during the Cultural Revolution). Though not particularly ancient, the teahouse provides entertainment over a pot of tea in fine old Beijing style (see the section *What to Do* for more on teahouses).

Medical Advice

Pushing on, we came to the **Tongrentang Traditional Medicine Shop**. A major outlet of herbal concoctions for the capital since 1669, Tongrentang was the official supplier of medicines to the imperial court during the reign of the Guangxu emperor (as decreed by the Empress Dowager Cixi).

Impressed by the ginseng root in the center glass case (12,000 *yuan* for a tiny wizened head that trails off into spidery threads), I asked the clerk about it:

Why is it so expensive?
It's the famous ginseng root from Jilin Province. (in northeast China)
Oh.
It's over fifty years old.
Ah.
It was dug up so that all these tiny hairs were saved, preserving its original fine shape.
I see...
It helps supplement the qi.
But who would pay so much?
Overseas Chinese and rich southerners. But look here, there's ginseng for everybody. (Pointing at the next case with ginseng slices, shavings, pills, capsules, and tea.)

Across the aisle was a selection of ingredients for Chinese traditional medicine—glass cases of seeds and leaves, dried sea horses and sea slugs, tiger bone, rhino horn, and snake wine. In the back gleamed the tall cabinets of a western medicine dispensary.

On our way out the door, we spotted an old man with a pinched face perched inside a booth. A line-up of advice seekers waited their turn to speak with the sage. In an unusual takeoff on the information counter theme, the retired doctor was listening to medical complaints and prescribing treatments from his ready supply of internalized experience. What a way to save on medical bills! But with socialized medicine, it's the time waiting in line at the hospital that's saved, not the money.

Shoes and Shows

Next door is the **Neiliansheng Shoe Store**, another business that's survived the centuries. A favorite among officials in the Qing Dynasty, the shop kept a careful record of boot sizes and preferred styles of its customers. A quick note sent down by courier ensured a pair of perfectly fitting boots in time for the next imperial proclamation. Court shoes went out of fashion with the court, but Neiliansheng stayed in business, using the layered soles it once used for boots to make popular flat cotton footwear.

Leather loafers and high-heeled pumps have been a way of walking for the Chinese since western products took over the fashion scene at the turn of the century. Today the all-black or all-white leather sports shoe is in, and hip Beijing youth let their high-top laces dangle. But for moderate walking, around the house, even biking, nothing beats the slip-on Chinese cloth shoe. There's no painful breaking-in period, and when one pair wears down, another costs just a couple of *yuan*. The basic black shoe is still popular, but a new range of colored, flowered, and embroidered styles for women have recently captured the market.

We strolled on until the shops petered out, past the first crumbling gateways and low roofs of Beijing's former red-light district. The brothels here were shut down in 1949 and the women shipped off to factories for reeducation and retraining. The area is now a quiet mix of homes and small guest houses, prostitution having moved on to bigger and better neighborhoods.

Turning back, we plunged again into the mob, passing the former **Acrobatic Rehearsal Hall**. The billing for that night was a video—a kung-fu cops and robbers flick. Some forms of amusement have changed; the places have not. During the Qing Dynasty, when a law was passed prohibiting "uproarious noise in the Inner City areas close to the Palace," party seekers were pushed south beyond the city gates. The Dazhalan area, with its five major playhouses, developed into the capital's prime entertainment center. Gentry, rich merchants, and nobility rickshawed down to watch plays and operas at theaters such as the Great Virtue Playhouse, their consorts for the evening ordered from one of the neighborhood brothels.

Bridge to Heaven

The ride down Qianmen Street to the Temple of Heaven (*Tiantan*) is not a biker's paradise. Like many streets in Beijing, it's a moving menagerie of the wheeled and walking. Pedi-cabs, the modern-day rickshaw, are pumped along by gray-haired grandpas toting tourists and harried businessmen. Produce carts, junk carts, three-wheeled motor scooters, tricycles (an adult version with a seat in back), and bicycles overflow into the car lane. Buses charge by at intervals, forcing the herd back across the line, squeezing it against the curb when they plow in for a drop-off.

We crossed the **Bridge of Heaven** (*Tianqiao*) intersection and continued on to the west gate of the temple. There was once a long white marble bridge spanning a river by the **Tianqiao Department Store**. The Emperor used to make his biannual excursion from the Imperial Palace to the Temple of Heaven along this route, crossing over the bridge and pulling in at the western gate. It's hard to imagine Beijing could ever observe a moment of silence, but back then, a dead hush was required for the solemn procession of nobles, officials, musicians, elephants, and horse chariots, dressed in their ritual best, that accompanied the Son of Heaven along this southern route to perform the most critical ceremonies of the year. Commoners (and foreigners) had to shutter themselves up inside to accomplish this great feat of silence.

The bridge and river are long gone, though remnants of old Beijing remain. Emperor Qianlong was the first to spruce up the area. He had the river landscaped with willows and red lotus. Before long, wine shops and teahouses sprang up along its banks. In the post-1911 Revolution period, when the Lotus Lane Market was relocated to this district, shops from seven different alleys moved here. Specialty stores sold imported fancies and the latest in time pieces. Second-hand shops dealt in clothes and hats. There were astrologers, fortune tellers, and theaters. Acrobats leapt and spun. Young toughs flexed and wrestled. Story tellers recited entire novels. "Doctors" sold miraculous elixirs.

The **Tianqiao Fortune Teahouse** (*Tianqiao Le Chayuan*), tucked away down a hutong across the street from the Tianqiao Theater, brings to life these colorful scenes from the past. A ticket at the door buys you a pot of tea, five tokens for snacks (sesame bun and roast pork sandwiches, innards soup, peanuts, a variety of sweet cakes, and almond paste dessert, among other delicacies) and a couple hours of good entertainment in a replica Qing Dynasty teahouse. Even without the language, you can enjoy the comedy acts, ballads, martial arts, and acrobatics. You can, as in days of old, sip your tea, crack sunflower seeds, chat with your neighbor, play Chinese chess, and spit on the floor.

Prayers to Heaven

The emperor, as Son of Heaven, acted as intermediary between the mortals under his guidance and Heaven above. He was responsible to Heaven, and he alone could perform the sacrificial rites necessary for keeping up good relations with the natural forces and ancestors. Natural disasters, bad harvests, and corruption (all of which so often coincided with bouts of bad government) indicated the loss of Heaven's mandate.

Once the emperor had fallen from heavenly grace, any peasant and his brother could organize an army to take on the imperial forces and establish a new legitimate dynasty. It was for this, if nothing else, that the Son of Heaven paid scrupulous attention to his dialogue with Heaven, a dialogue codified over the centuries into a precise formula of respectful ritual.

Shou and I pulled up at the **West Heavenly Gate** to buy our tickets. The Temple of Heaven is one tourist spot that has come under price reform in recent years. Everybody, regardless of nationality, used to pay just two *mao* for admission; now it's up to five *mao* for the Chinese, ten *yuan* FEC (Foreign Exchange Currency) for all others. The park opens at six every morning, closing late in the evening during the warmer months (April-September).

Entering from the west brought us directly to the **Hall of Abstinence** (*Zhaigong*). Here the emperor came the day before the winter solstice to purify himself by abstaining from contaminating substances, such as meat and women. The plaque inscribed with "Rules of the Fast" was kept on hand to remind him of his solemn duty. An Emperor Qianlong mannequin poses authoritatively on the throne near the back of the hall, but the blockade at the door, typical of Chinese museums, prevented closer inspection.

East through the pines, we came to the round **Altar of Heaven** (*Huanqiutan*) in the extreme south of the park. Conceived and constructed in 1530, the open-air altar looks like a three-tiered white marble cake. The flagstones underfoot sweep outward in concentric circles of nine multiples, from the center ring of nine on the top tier to the twenty-seventh ring at the bottom with 243 (twenty-seven times nine). Odd numbers, being associated with *yang*, were considered heavenly, and nine, being the highest single-digit odd number, ranked imperial.

The emperor came here at first light on the winter solstice to offer ritual sacrifice. Climbing the steps to the top tier symbolized ascent from the earth (the bottom layer), through the mortal world (the middle), to heaven at the highest point. There, in the center amidst swirls of incense smoke and tinkling bells, he performed the rites critical to his nation's well-being. His full morning schedule included sacrifice to the Supreme Ruler of the Universe, the spirits of the sun, moon, stars, clouds, rain, wind, thunder, and his own ancestors.

The ancestor tablets used in those rites were stored in the **Imperial Vault of Heaven** (*Huangqiongyu*) directly north. Engraved with the name, birth date, and date of death, wooden ancestor tablets are like portable tomb stones used to memorialize the deceased. Before the popularization of Confucianism in the late first century B.C., the emperor alone was responsible for worshipping the ancestors—his sacrifices to the heavenly deceased served as a full-cover national insurance policy.

Tablets aside, it is the circular **Echo Wall** enclosing the Vault that draws the crowds into the inner courtyard. Lean up against the inner curve, and you can talk to your partner thirty meters away, vision blocked by the central hall (both heads must be at the same altitude). There are also the **Echo Stones**, the three stone slabs leading up to the Hall. Stand on the first, clap your hands, and you get one echo. Step forward, clap again, and you'll have two. On to the third, and you'll have three.

Chinese Geometry

North along the **Bridge of Vermilion Steps** (merely a raised flagstone walkway), we came to the **Hall of Prayer for Good Harvests** (*Qiniandian*). The crowning glory of ancient Chinese architecture, it rises from the pines, a brilliant blue umbrella knobbed in gold. Here the Son of Heaven came twice a year to pray: on the fifteenth day of the first lunar month to ask for a good harvest, and at the winter solstice to give thanks for blessings received. The present building dates from only 1890. Its predecessor from 1420 was struck by lightning and burned to the ground.

Circles and squares predominate. The outer courtyard is square, the shape of the earth as determined during the Ming Dynasty. The temple itself is round—like Heaven. Look at the park on a map for an aerial impression. The southern edge lies flat like the earth; the line along the north bulges up into a Heavenly semi-circle.

The Hall of Prayer for Good Harvests is an architectural wonder. That tremendous blue—Heavenly blue—roof rests ingeniously atop wooden pillars without the benefit of a single nail. It is also a numerological delight where, again, odd numbers reign. Below is a triple-tiered round marble terrace, above three layers of blue-tiled roof. The wooden pillars supporting the roof are an exception: four in the middle represent the seasons, the twelve ringing those denote the months of the year. The outer twelve are the twelve "watches" of the day.

By the time we re-emerged, the sun was already flirting along the tree line, dropping long shadows of pine like oil slicks over the weedy turf. We pulled our bikes from the tangle at the gate and pushed off into the crowd of dinner seekers jostling north toward Qianmen Street.

Surreptitious Soy

There are two state-run vegetarian restaurants in Beijing—one south of Xidan on Xuanwumen Street and the other at 158 Qianmen. Both serve a luscious array of roast duck, steamed fish, fried chicken, and barbecued pork, all concocted from various makes and molds of soy.

Gongdelin lies just north of the Tianqiao intersection. Upstairs is somewhat preferable to the ground floor. Typically, the quality of food, decor, and service in state-run restaurants rises in its proximity to Heaven. Whereas chowing with the masses on the first floor entails options for slurping and spitting, upstairs dining is designed to be an esthetic, epicurean delight.

Though at Gongdelin such disparity is minimized, the top floor does offer a treetop view of the street.

I thought the place strangely empty for a Sunday evening. But as Shou reminded me, vegetarian cuisine, no matter how carefully disguised, is not a favorite among the carnivorous Chinese. Our fellow diners in the spacious, well-lit room consisted of a jovial party of Japanese and several pairs of courting couples along the back wall—sacrificing their meat to escape the crowds, no doubt.

Our seafood arrived first—a dish of braised eel and shrimp fried with cashews. This was followed by a plate of honest greens and mushrooms. All were swimming in grease, as is par for the vegetarian course. The cooks must want to make up for the lack of meat by an overdose of oil. Hot rice and cold beer neutralized the effect, making for a very enjoyable meal.

Red-light Runners

It had been a full day in the "Chinese City." Pulling back into Qianmen Street, we pedaled north past shops shuttered for the night. Dusk had already settled. It was one of those balmy spring evenings where you can taste the ripening summer, wish for it like the flesh of sweet watermelon piled on street corners under low-watt bulbs. A light wind ran softly, at our backs.

Following at the wheels of the crowd, neither of us was paying attention to what was going on around. We must have been deep in conversation. Suddenly there was a shout. I looked up to see a skinny, bespectacled traffic cop waving madly at us from his soapbox in the eye of the intersection. Curiosity drew us over—there was no telling what we'd done wrong.

Necks craned up at the cop, cars and buses skimming by, we learned that we'd just run a red light. There was no point in arguing that everybody in front of us had done the same, or that it was merely a front tire crossing the white line, or that *everybody* in Beijing runs red lights. We pulled our bikes in close and listened attentively in craned neck attitude, wondering how long the lecture would last.

It took several minutes for him to inspect our work cards and carry out a thorough investigation of our identity and intent, including my nationality and Shou's age and marital status. Satisfied at last, he released us with a wave of his hand, telling us how fortunate we were to get away without a fine. Our punishment turned out to be an elongated public display of guilt—no small matter in a culture preoccupied with saving face.

SUMMER

Imperial Parklands

From the Beijing Library west along Purple Bamboo Road to the canal; north to the Summer Palace, east to Yuanmingyuan and Beijing University, turning south along Baishiqiao Road to the Friendship Hotel.

A Slow Start

We knew we had to get out of the city to escape the heat. Summer in Beijing is hot—not the comfortable dry heat of California, but a slow, sticky greenhouse, where two showers a day doesn't suffice. Three friends and I, all long-term residents in China employed by the state-run foreign languages publishing house, decided one warm night that a bike trip into the hills was in order.

Animated discussion in Russo-Italian-English landed us with the following plan: We'd make a large loop—take the canal route up to the Summer Palace, turn east toward Yuanmingyuan and get back to the

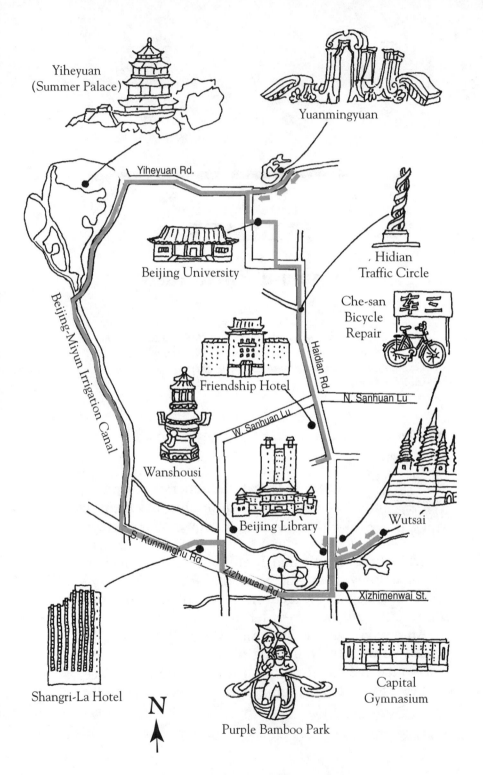

IMPERIAL PARKLANDS

Friendship Hotel for a dip in the pool before closing time.

The next morning, though hot and sunny, dawned relatively damp free. We met at the **Beijing Library** on Baishiqiao Road, where Sergio had gone earlier to look up some material for an article at work. When it was twenty minutes past the appointed time and still no Sergio, we decided to go in and drag him out.

Most institutions and schools in China are protected by a high stone wall or chain link fence. Bicyclists are typically asked to dismount and walk through the gate, a regulation enforced by a metal bar speed bump. Beijing Library, slightly ahead of its time, requires the dismount but does not press the point with an unwieldy obstruction. We parked in the covered lot skirting south along the fence edge. There's no car space—just row after row of two-wheelers, heavy black models interspersed with the occasional red or green. When you see them lined up, locked in place like cars in a parking garage, you understand the true mode of transportation in Beijing—at least for scholars who frequent the library.

The imposing front entrance to the largest book fortress in the country is always locked (like many front doors in China). We showed our I.D. cards to the guard at the side door and, for a time, left behind the noise, heat, and crowds. Tiptoeing through that spacious, carpeted, air-conditioned bubble of modernity, we finally located Sergio buried in the Italian section of the foreign languages reading room.

Though well stocked in all languages (16,864,829 volumes as of 1991), the library remains a hard nut to crack. Most of the holdings, hidden deep in its bowels, are lifted to the surface in the little trolley cars of a German tracking system. One book may take thirty minutes to appear. Library cards, issued only to those

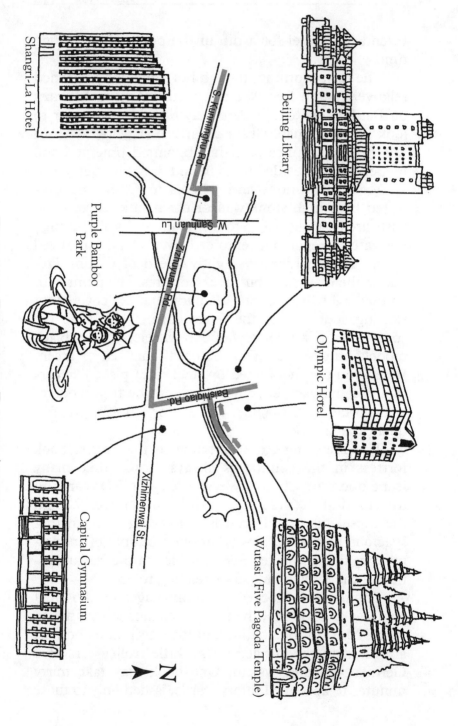

of the right professional rank, are strictly controlled through the work unit. Though hardly a lending library, the open-stack reading rooms (over thirty in all, with books and journals in every language) do offer accessible material and quiet space to the public.

Indian Import

Our second stop that day was through the **Five Pagoda Temple** (*Wutasi*). Sadia, an Indian import herself, had been going on about it for months, claiming it's one of the best places in Beijing, both for the pagodas and the collection of inscribed stone tablets that date back to the thirteenth century.

East along the canal road between the steel-blue **Olympic Hotel** and **Capital Gymnasium** brought us first to the **Municipal Indoor Ice Skating Rink**. It squats to the left like a huge grounded blimp. Rounding the corner, we found ourselves in a medieval stone farmyard, where rows of horses, lions and *Bixi* (tortoise-like animals) line the drive to the temple gate. The back entrance to **Beijing Zoo**, featuring live pandas, lies just over the canal bridge to the south—for those who like visiting animals behind bars.

The temple is an architectural anomaly. Set on a high square base (the throne), five pointed pagodas (the diamonds) rise above the trees to pierce the blue sky above. Sadia explained that an Indian monk introduced this "diamond throne pagoda" style to China in the early fifteenth century. Originally named the Temple of True Awakening (*Zhenjuesi*) at its founding in 1473, it's now simply called Five Pagoda Temple (*Wutasi*). There are only eight "diamond throne pagodas" in all of China, four of them in Beijing. The others are the Temple of the Azure Clouds (*Biyunsi*) in the Western Hills, the Yellow Temple (*Huangsi*) at Andingmen, and the Temple of High Excellence (*Miaogaosi*) at Jade Spring Mountain.

We passed through the small temple museum inside the base and climbed the winding staircase to get a close-up on the pagodas. Rusted bronze bells hang from the tips of their sloping, layered eaves. The collection of stone stelae below spreads like a giant chess game of white pieces over the grassy turf. These tablets, riding on the backs of *Bixi* or resting on square foundations, record three dynasty's worth of merits and virtues in a total of six hundred inscriptions.

From our perch on the roof (the flat top of the throne), the world appeared a wash of green. Poplar and willow smothered the cracks between tile and wall, covering the dirt and puffing up the earth with shoots of life. A place not to miss, the temple offers cool respite from the urban rush and grime. Its garden of stone lends a quiet, ageless grace requiring no translation.

Reputable Repair

Refreshed and ready for our trek into the hills, we clambered out the gate and back into the sun. But a quick getaway wasn't in the cards. Dmitry's back tire had taken advantage of our absence to relieve itself of internal pressure. There was nothing to do but walk our bikes up to the repair shop on Baishiqiao Road.

Che-san ("Bike-three") Bicycle Repair has gained some fame in the capital as the oldest and largest privately owned enterprise of its kind. To western eyes, it looks like a regular repair shop, perhaps a little more grease and a little less interior decoration, but the shop itself is an unusual phenomenon. Most repair in this bicycle town is accomplished by self-employed street-side entrepreneurs who work out of their tool carts by day and disappear by night. Che-san, on the other hand, never really closes. After six in the evening, there's a bell around the back for emergency night time fix-ups.

Look for the crowd of bikes in front. The shop itself, located across the street from the gaudy science and technology center north of the library, is a nondescript hole-in-the-wall. If you can't find it, ask. Everybody in the area knows about Che-san. "Boss," a friendly sort in his sixties (written up in *The San Francisco Chronicle*, as his wall of clippings testifies) wasn't in. His son, the new "boss," took care of us right away.

"Flat!" he yelled into the inner room.

A greasy lackey leaped up from the hulk he'd been working on and threw the bike on its back. Most people need about twenty minutes to repair a tube puncture. Give an expert five. With that fellow, it was a matter of seconds, and at the cost of only one *yuan*. Prices are fixed, and the work guaranteed. We took turns at the electric pump outside, filling up with last minute air. Finally, our journey was to begin.

Purple Bamboo

Doubling back, we turned west at the intersection by the **Capital Gymnasium**. A relic from the sixties, the gym prides itself on its huge seating capacity. I once had to leave a basketball game because I couldn't make out what was happening from my seat in the thirty-seventh row. It's that big. Ten minutes home by bike and I was able to catch the second half on TV.

The road follows along the southern edge of the **Purple Bamboo Park**. Passing the gate, we had to weave through a pack of vendors and hand-held children clutching balloons, paper pinwheels, and dripping ice cream. Excited shouts rang out over the blurred music of kiddie rides, whirring and bumping on the other side of the high park wall. Like parks citywide, the Purple Bamboo attracts a different crowd depending on the hour. Sunup brings the older set, retirees who enjoy a good stretch or sing in the morning. Daytime, especially on weekends, brings children and their parents to play. Finally, with the dusk, young lovers slink along the graveled paths and disappear into the bamboo groves.

The park lakes and **Changhe River** to the north swim with local history. During the Qing era, imperial parties boated up these waters on their way from the Forbidden City to the Summer Palace. A riverside villa was once conveniently located near the **Temple of Longevity** (*Wanshousi*), allowing Qing emperors and their retinues a mid-journey rest. All that remains of the villa is the landing dock. But the temple still stands, tucked down a lane northwest of the Purple Bamboo Park.

Wanshousi, built in 1577, is not considered a major tourist attraction. Like Wutasi to the east, the temple exudes a cracked and peeling beauty of old. Also, like Wutasi, it's a fine place to escape to when you've had your fill of the usual tourist fare. The **Beijing Art Museum**, with both a permanent collection and temporary exhibits of work by local artists, is housed in the inner courtyard.

The mammoth cloverleaf crossover at the intersection with the Third Ring Road (*Sanhuan Lu*), though a blessing to motorists, is a major obstruction in the life of a bicyclist. Forced to loop north for lack of a bike lane, we detoured through the back lot of the **Shangri-La Hotel**. This five-star high-rise is a regular hang-out for the foreign community in these parts. Unlike the ritzy east, where fancy hotels bump elbows on every block, the great western outback offers this one retreat into luxury.

When in Doubt, Haggle

There was little to obstruct our path on the long, straight stretch to the canal, only occasional Sunday riders more intent on the discussion at hand than any particular destination. We passed row after row of uninspired six-story apartment buildings fronted by a low curtain of tiny shops and restaurants. The lines throughout are squared, the colors flat. In summer, at least, there are trees to relieve that drab feeling—winter on a such street can be dismal.

Carts piled high with fresh summer fruit were lined up along the curb near the canal. Peaches, plums, tiny sour apricots, green apples, red berries, melons, and ever-present southern-grown bananas were our choices. All looked so good, it was difficult for the four of us to agree. We walked away with a big bag of the fragrant golden-pink peaches purchased from a round old woman and her bony husband after much discussion:

> Look, try these peaches. They're good!
> *They don't look ripe.*
> No! They're just right. Here, I'll cut one open so you can try. (cutting into the pink fruit with a hefty all-purpose knife)
> *Hmm... Not bad. How much for a jin?* (about one pound)
> Two **kuai**. (*kuai* is colloquial for ***yuan***)
> *Two **kuai**! That's way too much!*
> Well, how many *jin* do you want?

Depends how low you'll go.
One ***kuai*** *nine.*
One ***kuai*** *eight and we'll buy five* ***jin.***
Oh, alright.

It seems trivial to haggle over a few *mao*, but taken in the right spirit, it's a necessary part of the game. Their grins as we pulled away assured us they too were satisfied with the deal.

Alley Talk

Crossing the canal bridge to the western edge, we found ourselves suddenly in the countryside. Lush green fields, interrupted only by lean-to greenhouses, low storage sheds, and small distant factories, stretched to blue mountains (the Fragrant Hills). Pockets of children, shaded by trailing willows, clung to the steep banks of the canal. An occasional swimmer stroked easily with the brown current. Wiping away our sweat, we looked down enviously. But suspicious of the water's content, we pedaled northward.

Motorized traffic eventually thinned out, the relative quiet broken only by an occasional cargo truck, beating back our voices and blasting soot down our lungs. Narrow hutongs angling west into the mash of brick row houses murmured with midmorning activity. Sadia wanted to get a few pictures, so we parked our bikes for a quick prowl around.

Our intention was to stroll inconspicuously down the little tree-lined way, but even if Sergio hadn't knocked that basin of water off the stool, we wouldn't have gotten far without being spotted. Three ungainly westerners and a dark-skinned Indian call attention to themselves in the most cosmopolitan areas of town, not to mention secluded hutongs in the outskirts.

Sergio's unsuccessful attempts to right the basin were met by shrieks of laughter from the gathering circle of neighborhood children. A row of black and gray heads extended in unison from the line of doorways and, simultaneously registering the situation, hung tentatively in wide-eyed silence.

"*Dui bu qi*!" Sergio apologized to the basin's owner, sending the children into further uncontrolled fits of glee. The heads jerked to life. Apparently satisfied we meant no harm, some of the residents stepped over their low thresholds to get a closer look.

"What country ya from?" A white-haired granny took charge.

Sergio answered for the group and apologized again for good measure. Grinning, the granny stooped over and hoisted high the grimy toddler who'd been peering round her legs. "Look at the foreigners," she pointed benignly with her index finger.

Next came the questions—Are you students? What do you do here? How much money do you make? How old are you? Are you married? Which is better, China or America? Though overabundance of attention made further exploration impossible, Sadia was able to use the time well. While the three of us fielded questions from the crowd, she snapped the circle around, capturing their faces on film. We finally managed to break away and made it back to our bikes on the road.

The shady stretch south of the Summer Palace is my favorite along the canal strip. Willows lean, their rippling skirts skimming the bare backs of huddled lovers fresh from the cool green water. Sunlight strikes the earth in dotted glimmers, daubing a patchwork of light on dark. In the distance rise two stone bridges marking the park's edge, one a half-moon arch like a bow pulled taut, the other a low gentle swell.

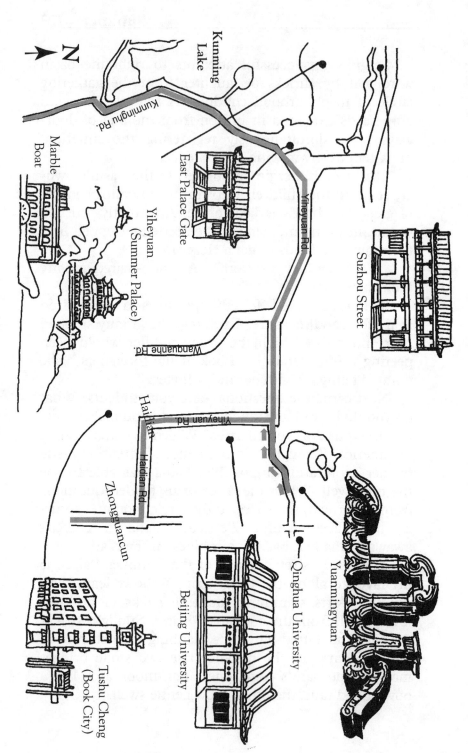

A flock of old men was crouched in clusters around metal cages of white rabbits and gray pigeons near the foot bridge. We wheeled our bikes across and pedaled north, following the high stone wall to the **New Palace Gate**. It is a longer walk to the central palace area from this side entrance, but traffic is much lighter here and easier to negotiate than around the main gate.

Park of Good Health and Harmony

Set on the edge of the Western Hills, **Park of Good Health and Harmony** (*Yiheyuan*) was the royal summer escape from Beijing's wilting heat for the better part of two centuries. As the "Summer Palace," it was built for both business and pleasure, combining court reception and living quarters with temples and parkland. **Kunming Lake**, modeled after the quiet beauty of West Lake in Hangzhou, covers about three-quarters of the total area.

The general layout of the park dates back about 800 years, when the first emperor of the Jin Dynasty moved his capital to the Beijing area and built his "Gold Mountain Traveling Palace" on this very spot. Seven hundred years ago, a Yuan Dynasty hydraulic engineer dug a riverbed (the present-day canal), channeling water from the north to bring grain into the capital. The pond at the foot of the hill thus grew into a large reservoir (the present-day lake). Then about 200 years ago, Emperor Qianlong of the Qing Dynasty set about developing the Western Hills into an imperial pleasure playground; his "Three Hills and Five Parks" stretched for over ten kilometers in its heyday. The **Summer Palace** (then called the "Park of Clear Ripples") was completed in 1764 for his beloved mother, after fifteen years of labor and 4.8 million taels of silver.

Like great cultural treasures the world over, the Summer Palace has been a favorite site for plundering invaders. French and English troops burned the place to the ground during the Second Opium War of 1860, leaving behind only nonflammables such as the **Marble Boat,** the **Bronze Pavilion,** and the lake. After the onslaught, the Empress Dowager Cixi pulled 30 million taels of silver from the royal coffers to enlarge and reconstruct. But her money was poorly spent. In 1900, Western troops stationed in China, angered by the Boxer Rebellion, demolished what they could of the newly installed treasures and ran off with the rest. Unwilling to accept defeat when it came to her own comfort, Cixi was at it again two years later, to the tune of 40,000 taels of silver a day.

Once she had the Summer Palace back in style, Cixi kept up her flamboyant standards. When she traveled by land, twelve hundred musicians and eunuchs on horseback were required to accompany her and Emperor Guangxu (the second to last emperor of the Qing Dynasty) from the Forbidden City. In terms of dining, eight courtyards of kitchens prepared 128 different culinary delights for every meal. She spent most of her later years at the Summer Palace, using it is a resort and secondary imperial palace until her death in 1908.

After the Revolution of 1911, the Summer Palace was allowed to stay in the hands of the Qing imperial family. Puyi, the last emperor, opened it to the public in 1914, but at a price few could afford. When he was run out of town in 1924, the Beijing Municipal Government took over. Maintenance was ignored, and over the next twenty-five years, the palace fell into disrepair. Some of its most valuable treasures were carted away by the Kuomingtang when they fled the mainland for Taiwan in 1949.

The restored Summer Palace we see today is the result of further dippings into the government purse. Its halls and towers are kept up but not overdone. Its paths, especially those on the north side of **Longevity Hill,** wind lazily through ancient groves (on a quiet off-season day you can find a solitary retreat). Its extensive lake area provides recreational variety: boating, swimming, fishing (even wind surfing), and ice skating in the winter.

Halls and Walls

Kunming Lake glistened in the mid-morning sun, its bobbing face thrashed to waves under the rows of exuberant boaters. **South Lake Island,** connected by the **Seventeen Arch Bridge,** and Longevity Hill at our right swarmed like anthills with busy tourists.

We visited first the **Hall of Benevolent Longevity** (*Renshoudian*), acting state headquarters when the court moved to the Summer Palace. Originally called the "Hall for Encouraging Good Government" at its restoration in 1890, the name was later changed to indulge Cixi's preoccupation with long life. A bronze menagerie of lions, dragons, phoenixes and *qilin* (a legendary beast with a dragon's head, lion's tail, deer's antlers, and ox's hooves, covered in fish scales) decorates the front terrace.

The **Garden of Harmonious Virtue** (*Deheyuan*) features an unusual outdoor opera stage. Five times larger than average, it's built in three levels, with traps in the ceiling and floor for immortals to swoop down from above and ghosts to rise from the underworld below. At Cixi's annual birthday celebration, the same opera would be performed simultaneously on all three levels. Underground tanks provided water for the "wet" scenes.

West along the lake are the residential courtyards. The small dock behind Cixi's **Hall of Joyful Longevity** (*Leshoudian*) allowed easy access for boating excursions and royal barge drop offs.

Emperor Guangxu was housed in the **Hall of Jade Ripples** (*Yulantang*). The pock-marked courtyard floor testifies to his days of house arrest after having supported the Reform Movement of 1898. Day in and day out he paced, tapping his walking stick in frustrated protest. Matters weren't helped by the fact that the gate to the adjoining women's quarters, the **Hall of Pleasing Rue** (*Yiyungong*), were bricked up as well.

We eventually came to the **Long Corridor** (*Changlang*). Finding definition in numbers, the Chinese are forever sharing information about height, width, length, weight, and square meters covered. Superlatives, as a result, take on great significance. The Long Corridor is not only long, it's the longest in Chinese garden architecture—skirting the lake shoreline for a full 728 meters (almost half a mile). Colorful scenes from classical novels and history painted on the crossbeams above the walkway bring to life Chinese tales from the distant past. We joined the bumping tourists in the covered corridor for a short stretch before turning off to climb the **Hill of Long Life**.

Longevity Hill

There are quieter paths, but we followed the main drag, the staircased, corridored complex of temples built like steps up the slope. Passing through the palaces where Cixi held her birthday extravaganzas, we came to the **Tower of Buddhist Fragrance** (*Foxiangge*). A high admittance fee keeps the place relatively crowd free.

Downstairs there's a huge gold-plated bronze Buddha. On the top floor of the tower is a narrow balcony that affords a panoramic view of the environs—a good view certainly, but not superior to the free look from the hill around back. To the south was the boat-dotted lake, shimmering like a dish of silver fire under the sun's hot rays. In the distance we could see scattered clumps of high-rises poking like concrete weeds from the dusty plain.

Down at water's edge, concealed by the trees, lies the infamous **Marble Boat**. Restored in 1888 with money reserved for the construction of a modern navy, this monument to misappropriation remains permanently docked at the western end of the Long Corridor. The Empress Dowager herself designed the two-story, steamship-style cabin. Large mirrors and stained glass windows set the tone for elegant lakeside dining.

The south face of the hill is dotted with pavilions and scenic rest stops, brandishing names to capture the imagination: **Revolving Scripture Repository, House of Leisure, Nest of Pines and Clouds, Strolling Through Painting Hall** (standing on the verandah, you are meant to feel like a brushstroke in a landscape painting). Imagine yourself, after a grueling 128-course lunch, retiring to the breezy shade of the **Hall of Limitless Pleasure** for a cup of tea.

The Western Hills

To the west of the Summer Palace lie the **Western Hills**. Their summer green gathered, pinched, and rolled as far as we could see. Jutting from their midst atop **Jade Spring Mountain** is the **Pagoda of Supreme Height**. It's said that Qing Dynasty emperors relied on the clear water gurgling from a natural spring there to quench their royal thirst.

Further on, enclosed by a high stone wall, is **Fragrant Hills Park** (*Xiangshan*), one of the former imperial hunting grounds. Its dense tree cover makes for an ideal summer escape. Most Chinese, however, finding comfort in crowds, wait for autumn to view the red maples, packing the park with more bodies than the trees themselves. Climbing to the summit at that time is preferable to the cable-car squeeze. Two enormous boulders on the ridge are said to resemble incense burners. These and the clouds of mist on a blurry day have given the park its imaginative name—the Fragrant Hills.

The **Temple of the Reclining Buddha** (*Wofosi*), backed up against the hill directly north, can be reached by a tiny choo-choo train that works its way through the **Botanical Gardens**. Story has it that the original Tang Dynasty recliner, cut from a sandalwood trunk, was burned in a fire. The model we see stretched out today is the work of Yuan Dynasty engineers who melted down fifty tons of copper for the project. Glass cases lining the Buddha's hall display the embroidered shoes presented by Qing Dynasty royalty to the bare-footed giant. The sal-trees outside, reminiscent of Sakyamuni's entry into Nirvana (Sakyamuni spoke last to his disciples while sitting under a sal-tree), were brought from India at the temple's founding.

Nearby lies the most stunning temple complex in the Beijing area, the **Temple of Azure Clouds** (*Biyunsi*). Built as a nunnery in 1366, it was expanded in the eighteenth century with the **Hall of Five**

Hundred Arhats and a **Diamond Throne Pagoda** (the same style as Wutasi). Six steps of ornate halls climb the slope to a crowning white marble pagoda on the summit. Sun Yat-sen's coffin was kept here until 1929 during construction of his memorial hall in Nanjing. Sun's clothes and hat remain sealed inside.

Mount Miaofeng, the highest peak in these parts, rises 1,300 meters above the sea. Far to the south, scattered through wooded valleys, can be found the **Eight Great Temples** (*Badachu*) and **Cherry Vale Garden** (*Yingtaogou*), a secluded park hidden away in a mountain crevice. All make excellent day bike trips.

The North Face

The north side of Longevity Hill has a wild, unkept feeling compared to the cramped, cultured south. We clambered down rocky paths to the broad sunstruck terrace of an imposing Tibetan-style temple. Mock window frames raised softened squares of peeling dusty rose from the glaring white-washed walls. Taking refuge in a strip of shade near the terrace edge, we looked out over the knobby green hills and open plaza leading to Suzhou Street below.

Suzhou Street, a fabricated city inside the Summer Palace grounds, was once the playground of princes and princesses, consorts, and concubines. During the Qing Dynasty, when the imperial family made their annual summer retreat into these hills, entertainment had to be found to keep away the palace blues. This simulated city allowed residents all the thrills of commercial urban life in the safety of their own home. Court eunuchs played the part of shopkeepers, shouting and carrying on (as shopkeepers did in those days) when a "customer" approached.

Demolished with the rest of the palace in 1900, Suzhou Street underwent massive restoration in recent years and is now open to the tourist horde. Teahouses, wine shops, bookstores, and antique shops once again line its narrow creek.

Our picnic destination was a shady grove near the **Pagoda of Many Treasures** (*Duobaota*). We followed a dirt path through the pines to the grounds of the tower, where silence, a forgotten pleasure, reigned. Glazed tiles on the pagoda roof sparkled in the sun. The terrace where monks used to pace, counting their beads in meditation, grinned a half-circle around the vacant foundations of the crumbled temple walls.

Stretching out on the grass, we devoured our well-traveled lunch. Ham and cheese sandwiches, washed down by warm beer, were followed by peaches. Quiet settled over the grove as we were eventually lulled into half sleep. But our siesta was not destined to be—mosquitoes, delighted to find four defenseless victims, had already begun their attack. Slapping our wrists and thighs, we beat a hasty retreat over the hill, through the courtyards, around the lake, and out the gate.

Shopper's Paradise

Turning north on Kunminghu road, we pedaled lazily past fields and fish ponds until suddenly, rounding a corner, we found ourselves in Grand Central Station (the main Palace gate). The fish ponds and ripening fields melted into a row of awkward, dirty restaurants. Corralled public buses, lined up like patient cattle, and careening mini-vans with shouting attendants, vied for the business of town-bound passengers.

Roadside vendors were hard at it, their wares—gaudy "silk" scarves, plastic toys, imported cigarettes, stone balls for improving health—arranged colorfully across makeshift carts and stands. You can find there Summer Palace paraphernalia for every occasion: T-shirts, ashtrays, fountain pens, key chains, watches, cards, posters—the possibilities are endless.

We passed under the huge gold memorial archway (*pailou*) marking the front of the Summer Palace. I noticed that the little alley with curving tile roofs and carved stonework that once cut to the north along the street had disappeared. In its place was a major thoroughfare. There's no shortage of restaurants in this area. "Little Red Lips Restaurant" looks like all the other dozens of simple eateries, but its name, painted in sloppy red, deserves an honorable mention for creativity. Left at the next stoplight brought us right on course to the **Park of Perfection and Brightness**, commonly known as Yuanmingyuan.

Palace turned Park

Part of the "Three Hills and Five Parks" imperial pleasure playground, Yuanmingyuan (a conglomerate of three smaller gardens) was built in the early and middle years of the Qing Dynasty. Five Qing emperors, from Yongzheng to Xianfeng, spent the greater part of the year at Yuanmingyuan (like Cixi with her Summer Palace), holding audience and conducting affairs of state. Administrative offices duplicating those in the Forbidden City made Yuanmingyuan the ruling center of the empire for over a hundred years.

The spacious rolling parkland, once crowded with brightly painted palaces, gilded halls, towers, and pavilions, must have once rivaled the Summer Palace. It's now a tranquil reserve of open meadows, rice fields, and wooded slopes. In 1860, British and

French commanders determined to punish the Qing emperor for "xenophobic" policies with a good plundering of his favorite park. They made a few choice hauls of the goods for Queen Victoria and Napoleon III before letting their troops at it, then left the place a smoldering heap of ashes.

Cixi went in to restore and remodel in 1879, but it wasn't long before foreign troops returned. The second blow, in 1900, nailed the lid on the park coffin. The site became a free-for-all rubble outlet for officials, merchants, peasants, and anybody who had an interest in the old building stones, tiles, and unburned wood. Even the ancient trees were cut down and the rocks lining the lake carted away.

When the plunderers got through, all that was left were the Western-style marble palaces built by Emperor Qianlong. The Jesuits employed in his court had drawn up the plans and, in 1745, oversaw the construction of little rococo palaces with horseshoe staircases, fountains, and a maze—a touch of Versailles in the Middle Kingdom. The only details distinctly Chinese were the glazed color tiles decorating the roofs and walls. Though the tiles have long been spirited away, these white marble skeletons still lie in a jumbled, photogenic heap in the northeast corner.

Yuanmingyuan was opened to the public after 1949. The grounds were cleared, paths and bridges repaired, and some of the rococo ruins reassembled. Rumor has it more redo is in the works.

Cool Retreat

Yuanmingyuan is an ideal park for the cyclist. Unfortunately, bikes are only allowed in the winter months, when crowds are thin and paths vacant. We left our bikes at the front gate and entered on foot.

Passing through the heavily touristed southern section, we found a narrow tree-lined lane that cut into the farmland heart of the park. Tenuous birch trees shaded the pond swimming with lotus and frogs. Plump stalks of green rice waited knee-deep in watery beds. We left the lane and scrambled across to the dirt spine between paddies, slipping over the moist earth, to a narrow footpath leading straight for a wall of trees. Inside the grove, it was cool and dark and damp, a refreshing oasis from the blaze outside. Two farmers in bright cotton tank tops reclined in the shade, their straw hats pulled low; another squatted nearby smoking a cigarette.

Seeing that we were setting up base, the squatter put out his cigarette and turned a curious eye on us. I held up a piece of fruit, but though his face broadened to pleased surprise, he waved away my offer. When Sergio pressed the point, getting up to put the peach in his hand, the farmer was forced to accept. Hat shoved back, he sidled over with his crumpled pack of cigarettes and squatted down beside us.

Peach juice flew, white smoke billowed. When the snoozers awoke, they told us their story: Laborers from Anhui Province (in the south), they'd come to make extra cash until harvest time when they'd return to their families. The squatter claimed to be forty-two, but with that sun-beaten, wrinkled face, he looked way over fifty. His daughter, he said, had come along to work as a housekeeper for a family in town. The others were both in their early twenties but could've passed for sixteen. Conversation slowed, and we got up to go. Brushing the dirt from our shorts, we departed reluctantly into the sun-swathed fields.

Rococo Ruins

From scattered young pines to paved walkway, our path led us north to the tumbled ruins of Qianlong's marble palaces. There, in halls of splendor, the emperor and his consorts used to lounge on imported couches, listening to Western music, dining on Western food, and playing with European toys. Primary activities nowadays are posing and snapping pictures around the crumbling white marble columns.

Slightly to the west is another amusement that has been recently reconstructed for twentieth century gropers. A small admittance fee will allow you to blunder through the twists and turns of a seventeenth century European-modeled maze in the heart of China. Emperor Qianlong used to install himself in the raised center pavilion on the night of Mid-Autumn Festival. From there he could enjoy the spectacle of his court ladies, a torch in each of their dainty hands, puzzle their way into the middle. A prize awaited the lucky first comer.

We walked on to Fuhai (Sea of Happiness) Lake in the western section. White swan paddle-boats and bobbing rowboats enhanced the sparkling blue. Most of the big parks in town offer such a lake and, for a small deposit and several *yuan* per hour, boats to coast around in. The breeze off the water was tempting, but we still had a dip in the Friendship Hotel pool before closing time.

University Row

Colleges and universities dominate the northwest corner of the city. Moving up College Road (*Xue Yuan Lu*) from the south, there's the Institute of Post and

Telecommunications, the University of Politics and Law, Beijing Medical University, the University of Aeronautics and Astronomics, the University of Science and Technology, and the Beijing Language Institute. Hang a left to the west, and you'll come to **Qinghua University** and renowned **Beijing University**.

Qinghua lies at the end of the road by Yuanmingyuan. The campus was part of an old imperial park converted into a prep school in 1911 for students selected to study in the United States on scholarship. Granted university status in 1928, this so-called "Chinese M.I.T." now has sixteen departments, heavy on engineering, and a nuclear research institute. The campus has retained its park-like ambiance. Trees, meadows, streams, and potted flowers make it a nice place for an afternoon stroll.

Beijing University (*Beida*), China's most widely acclaimed institution of higher education, fills the halls of the former American Methodist Yenching University. Moved to the northwest corner of town in 1952 from its downtown campus, Beida (known as Capital College until the Revolution of 1911) was the sole survivor of Emperor Guangxu's modernization program of 1898. The list of women and men who have studied and taught at this school is like a Who's Who of modern Chinese history. Mao Zedong himself spent a couple years sorting books in the library.

Sadia had to stop by and see a friend on the Beida campus. We approached the gate along a leafy side street where the high gray wall stood sheathed in shade. Dismounting as required, we were waved through by the uniformed guard into the school's western domain. The cluster of buildings straight ahead, built in the early 1900s, are remnants of the Yenching University era. Their gracefully curved eaves speak of a time before the Soviet architects arrived to flatten and codify, sucking life from the angles and surfaces.

The Beida campus is particularly appealing in the warmer months when flowers are in bloom, the leaves and grass plump with dew. Our winding way took us along a stream that spilled into a small lake of pink lotus and leaning willows. Afternoon rays spun a web of silvery light around floating green pads. Young couples reclined on the grassy bank sharing awkward first moments.

Just past the lake we turned into the courtyard of the foreign students' enclave—a world unto itself of residence halls, offices, classrooms plus a dining room, laundry, sundry shop, and a long distance telephone office—a world of convenience designed to keep foreign guests a safe distance from China. While Sadia ran in to find her friend, we filled the time by watching a couple of Japanese students dart busily over the adjoining tennis court. Dressed impeccably in the latest sports wear, signature racquets in hand, they slashed and swept furiously under the burning sun. Just to watch was exhausting.

High-tech Nomenclature

Exiting via the south main gate, we passed rows of solidly built, but dilapidated dormitories. Student housing in China is pathetic—four or five bunk beds pushed up against peeling walls, bits of cloth strung along the edge of each bed for visual privacy, a couple communal tables and stools for in-room study. It's like summer camp for children, but all year around. Personal space, without even a set of drawers for storage

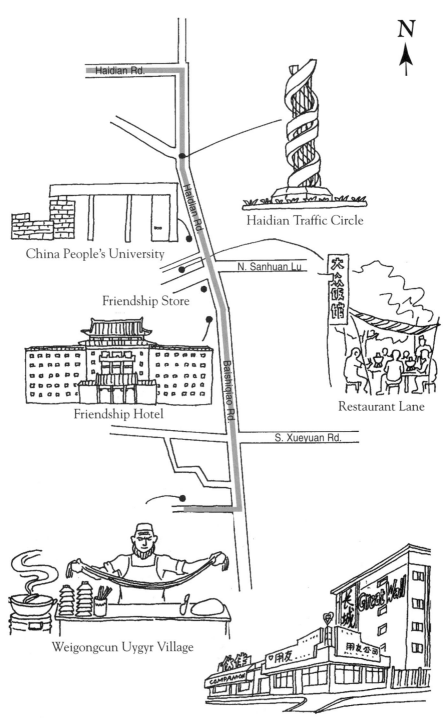

WEIGONGCUN

or a bookcase to call one's own, takes on new meaning under such conditions.

We cut east through **Haidian**, a loose-ended shopping district that serves Beida and the surrounding community. West along that road would have brought us to the newly completed **Book City** (*Tushu Cheng*) outdoor shopping mall, a lane of multiple-story book outlets crowded through the day with vegetable vendors, notions stands, and beverage carts.

Haidian Road, south of Beida, is the Silicon Valley retail strip for this part of the world. Every major enterprise that deals with computers and related high-tech equipment in Beijing is represented here. Orange and blue tape festoons the windows of each shop front, announcing the latest arrivals and good buys. Strange combinations of ill-matched letters are strung together to form words like "BXHDN" or "HDJQFD." Don't think the Chinese are inventing a new vocabulary—it's just their way of condensing exasperatingly long shop names into an easy handful of initials (based on the pronunciation of each character). This phenomenon can be observed on shop fronts all over the city.

Southward we rode, slowing for the milling throng outside **People's University**, where shoppers, sellers, eaters, and lookers had gathered in their usual late afternoon profusion. Small, privately-owned restaurants in that area have learned how to please their summer customers. Dinner tables were already spread, some more precariously than others, across the uneven turf, and where the pinched lanes ran, pushed tight against the walls. An evening under the trees with a cold drink and good friends will bring you back to these tables for more.

Home Again

The "**Friendship Store**" at the next corner (not to be confused with the big one downtown) marked our return home. Having recently undergone a facelift, this shop has taken on new status in the Haidian area. Its shelves are stocked with imported cigarettes, liquor, and candy. Imported beauty care products, stationery, and underwear fill the shining glass cases in back. But unlike the "Friendship Store" downtown, which is still largely populated by the foreign crowd, local Chinese fill its aisles and compete for attention.

We pulled into the **Friendship Hotel** next door, home to Beijing's horde of "foreign experts" and an increasing number of small, private businesses. Built in the fifties to house Soviet experts and their families, this hotel is really much more. It's a mammoth complex of apartment buildings, tourist accommodations, and a range of facilities to ensure comfort in every corner: coffee shop, roof-top bar, theater, expert's club, bakery, dry goods store, clinic, hair salon, full-sized swimming pool, and tennis courts. Much like the foreign students' compound at Beida, once you're inside, there's no reason to leave.

The pool was crowded. Sizzling red and brown bodies of every nationality stretched along side. Paler folk and Chinese women concerned with preserving their delicate skin hid themselves under the awning. We plunged into the water, shedding layers of accumulated heat in the chlorinated blue. The pool is open every day in summer from 12 to 6 pm and from 7 to 10 pm. An indoor pool takes over in the winter months.

A Real Meal

Refreshed by our swim, our minds turned naturally to our stomachs. There are a handful of home-style Chinese diners across the road, but our undisputed choice for a good meal was Xinjiang noodles.

Weigongcun, a short bike ride south from the Hotel, is one of two major Uyghur communities in this part of town, the other located in the Baiwanzhuang area west of Ganjiakou. Turning right off Baishiqiao Road, we followed the dusty hutong past fresh produce stalls, brick hovels that serve as homes, and tiny, patioed restaurants where women in bright scarves sell round flat bread fresh from the oven.

This neighborhood has a texture, taste and smell all its own. The Uyghurs hail from Xinjiang, a large piece of real estate in the northwest corner of China. They do not look like Han Chinese, resembling rather their relatives across the border in Middle Asia. Nor do they eat like the Hans. Their food, owing to Islamic regulation, is heavy on the mutton and devoid of pork. Shish-kabob, flat baked bread, and Xinjiang noodles (doughy noodles smothered with a tomato-based vegetable and mutton stew) are the most popular dishes to have entered the capital.

We pedaled past the first six or seven diners. Oversized tape decks blared Uyghur pop hits and traditional tunes to the customers seated outside. Each serves nearly the same food, and all have their bad days. Mohammed's place at the far end of the lane is as good as any. Seating ourselves at the rickety table in a strip of shade, we ordered a cucumber salad, noodles, and beer. Hot tea, as is the Uyghur custom, arrived first. As we sat talking to Mohammed, the sky slowly peeled back its afternoon glare and deepened into evening.

What To See

Beijing, capital of the Chinese empire for almost six centuries, is a city of historical landmarks, imperial remains, and cultural coffers. There's enough within the city limits to keep even the most industrious tourist busy for weeks. Naturally all the interesting places to visit cannot be adequately covered in a book of this length. Two of the most popular sites, the Forbidden City and the Great Wall, as well as a number of museums and centers of religious pursuit not mentioned in the bike trips, are introduced below.

The Forbidden City

Though it could be included on a bike trip, the Forbidden City, five hundred-year-old home to the Ming and Qing emperors, requires a good half day of exploration. After tramping around its courtyards and corridors, you'll probably want to digest what you've seen over a cold beer or hot cup of tea rather than race off for more. (Bicycles unfortunately aren't allowed inside, though Puyi, the last Qing emperor, remodeled his home by sawing off some to facilitate two-wheeled transport). The Forbidden City and Imperial Palace Museum are open every day but Monday, 8:30 am to 5 pm. Audio tour-packs are available and recommended, unless you can attach yourself to a guided tour in the language of your choice. Do not do like the fashionable Chinese—totter over the flagstones in high heels. Wear a pair of good walking shoes to cover that great expanse of formerly forbidden ground.

The Imperial Palace was for centuries the center of the world to the Chinese. It was here the Son of Heaven (the emperor) sat on the Dragon Throne and ruled the Middle Kingdom (*Zhongguo*). As holder of the Heavenly Mandate and thus intermediary between Heaven and earth, he was responsible for earthly peace, harmony, and prosperity. The symmetrical design of the palace reflects this ideal of hierarchical order. Aligned on a north-south axis, the key buildings face the sun, the origin of life and provider of all, in the south.

Emperor Yongle of the Ming Dynasty (and his million laborers and craftsmen) established the basic layout between 1406 and 1420. The Manchus set it ablaze in 1664, then rebuilt their own quarters along the same lines. In the 20th century alone, the Japanese have been in for a looting, and in the weeks before the Communist takeover of 1949, the Kuomingtang emptied out thousands of crates worth of goods. Air-lifted to Taiwan, the haul was so complete that even after more than forty years of rotating exhibitions at the Palace Museum in Taipei, most still remains packed away in the bomb-proof basement. The Kuomintang left little behind but the walls. The majority of the antiques and art objects in the Imperial Palace Museum's eight hundred buildings and 9,000 rooms have been carted in from around the country to make up for the loss.

You can enter from any direction: north, south, east, or west. It makes most sense to begin at the southern main entrance by Tian'anmen Square—the

Meridian Gate (*Wumen*)—and work your way through the Front Palace area to the Inner Palace in the north. The emperors, on their rare excursions to the great outdoors, used the central passage of the Meridian Gate. Officials and relatives were restricted to the side openings (west for the military; east for civilians).

The Imperial Palace is divided into an Outer Court and Inner Court. The Hall of Supreme Harmony (*Taihedian*), Hall of Complete Harmony (*Zhonghedian*) and Hall of Preserving Harmony (*Baohedian*) form the heart of the Outer Court. The Hall of Supreme Harmony, as the throne room, was reserved for the most important state ceremonies: coronations, celebration of New Year's Day and the emperor's birthday, announcement of successful candidates in the imperial examinations, and proclamation of imperial directives. Directly to the north, the Hall of Complete Harmony served as the emperor's lounge. He stopped here to make last minute preparations, rehearse ceremonies, and meet with close ministers. The Hall of Preserving Harmony was used for banquets and imperial examinations.

The Inner Court was the emperor's domestic quarters and the center of real power. The Palace of Heavenly Purity (*Qianqinggong*), home to emperors from the Ming through to the Kangxi emperor of the Qing, was later used as an audience hall for receiving foreign envoys. On both sides lie the East and West Palaces, where the emperor thrived as the only adult male with his family of concubines, children, eunuchs, serving women and the empress. Ten thousand people were living in the palace as late as 1900. Near the northern gate is the Imperial Garden, once the only natural refuge for palace inmates. It is a fine example of how traditional Chinese landscape design manipulates artificial rocks, pavilions, twisted trees, and bamboo into a harmonious whole.

The Great Wall

The Great Wall is a dragon across the northern reaches, winding and buckling over the hills. It is a determined barrier of stone and earth fortified with the bones of manual laborers, and a symbol of national definition and defense. The Great Wall, *Wan Li Chang Cheng* (the Wall of Ten Thousand *Li)* stretches 3,946 miles (6,350 km) from the Bohai Sea to the Gobi Desert. It is the only construction that American astronauts on their first flight to the moon could recognize with the naked eye. It's high enough to deter the northern nomads, wide enough to ride horseback six abreast. It's tremendous, colossal, amazing. It's the world's longest wall.

Sections of the wall were built by farming folk settled in the Yellow River basin in the Warring States Period to deter invaders from the north. Qin Shi Huang, the first emperor of a unified China (221-210 B.C.), in a step aimed at pulling the drawstring even closer, had them patched together and revitalized into a single defensive bulwark. The Wall stood right on through the 14th century, but its effectiveness was greatly reduced by greedy sentries who put personal gain before national security. During the Ming Dynasty, when danger of a Mongol invasion loomed, fortification of the wall became a matter of life and death. Fired brick was used to reinforce the original earth base; the fortified towers and garrisons were extended and developed.

The Wall today is back to bits and pieces stage, thanks to time and the natural elements. Though several sections have been renovated for public viewing, much of the winding dragon has been worn down to a crumbling snake. The Beijing area offers glimpses of both; Badaling, Mutianyu, and Gubeikou are the most commonly visited spots to date.

Public transportation is available, but a bike ride to Badaling, the closest and most commonly visited section of the Wall, is also a possibility. Some worthy stalwarts have pumped the seventy kilometers (about forty miles) from Beijing, and others, choosing a compromise, have brought bikes with them on the train to explore the surrounding mountain areas.

Museums

Museums in China require patience and good vision. If you can get past the awkward presentation and poor lighting, there are some real gems to be found. Bring a Chinese-speaking friend to help with the translation; English explanations are scarce in all but the biggest galleries. Hours usually run 9 am to 5 pm, with Monday often taken as a holiday.

History

Museum of Chinese History and Museum of the Revolution
East side of Tian'anmen Square.

Imperial Palace Museum
Inside the Forbidden City.

Former Residence of Soong Qingling
North Heyan Street; in the Houhai area.

Imperial Historical Archives
Nanchizi Street; east side of the Forbidden City.

Capital Museum
Guozijian Street; inside the Confucian Temple.

Museum of Ancient Astronomical Instruments
Jianguomen traffic circle; inside the Beijing Observatory.

Art and Culture

National Art Gallery
Corner of Wusi Street and Wangfujing Street.

Minorities Cultural Palace
Fuxingmennei Street; east of the Fuxingmen subway stop.

Former Residence of Lu Xun (writer)
North Funei Street; west of Xisi intersection.

Former Residence of Mei Lanfang (Beijing Opera star)
Baoguosi Street; near Ping'anli.

Former Residence of Qi Baishi (painter)
Kuache *Hutong*, West City District

Former Residence of Xu Beihong (painter)
North Xinjiekou Street; near Xinjiekou.

Former Residence of Mao Dun (writer)
Houyuan'ensi Street, Jiaodaokou

Science

Museum of Chinese Agriculture
North Dongsanhuan Road, Sanlitun

Museum of Natural History
Tianqiao area; just opposite the Tianqiao Department Store.

Beijing Planetarium
Xizhimenwai Street; across the street from the zoo.

Geological Museum
Yangrou Lane; at the Xisi intersection.

Military Museum
Fuxingmenwai Street; west of the Fuxingmen subway stop at Muxidi.

Temples, Mosques, Churches

Beijing has long been a focal point of religious endeavor. Buddhism from India, Islam from the Middle East, Christianity from the West, and Daoism from the heart of China, have all played a part in developing this cosmopolitan capital of the Middle Kingdom. Temples, mosques and churches, enclaves of culture in their own right, dot the skyline with their pagodas and domes and spires. Most were closed down and well battered during the Cultural Revolution (1966-1976), but they are now open again and breathing with renewed vigor.

Buddhism

Strictly speaking, Buddhism is not a religion, since it is not centered on a god, but a philosophy and code of morality. Based on the teachings of Siddhartha Gautama, known as Sakyamuni, who lived in India around 500 B.C., Mahayana ("large vehicle") Buddhism traveled overland to China in the first century A.D. Cycles of proliferation and persecution followed the imperial whim, and the Chinese developed several flavors of Buddhist philosophy and practice to suit their own tastes. Chan Buddhism (*Zen* in Japanese), with some similarities to Daoism, is the most well-known. All the various schools of Buddhist thought share a single aim: to reduce the suffering caused by human desires.

There are several tiers of divine beings in the Chinese pantheon. At the top are those who have achieved perfection and live in Nirvana, the Buddhas. The most important of these is Sakyamuni, sitting in meditation or lying down, generally the central figure in one of several Buddha trinities. The trinity of three ages has Sakyamuni (Shijiamouni), Buddha of the Present; Kasyapa (*Jiayefo*), Buddha of the Past; and Maitreya (*Milofo*), Buddha of the Future. Chan temples often match Sakyamuni with Amitabha (*Emitofo*) and Bhaisajyaguru (*Yaoshifu*, the god of medicine).

Bodhisvattas at the second level have remained in the world to relieve suffering and lead the rest of the flock to salvation. Maitreya, the Bodhisvatta of the Future, is known in the West with his broad smile and broader belly as the "Laughing Buddha." Guanyin, the Goddess of Mercy, is a popular bodhisvatta native to China.

Finally come the arhats, the immortals who've been ordered to stay in this world and preach the Buddhist doctrines. Eighteen or so line up on either side of the Buddhas in the main hall. Tutelary gods, guardian spirits, and patriarchs of the various sects appear in the back and side halls.

Buddhist temples look like fortresses. Surrounded by high, thick walls, a few south-facing central halls padded by inner courtyards are flanked on either side by buildings of lesser importance. In the first hall sits Maitreya, protected by the four heavenly kings in front and Veda (*Weito*), guardian of Buddism, in back. Three Buddhas (one of the trinities) occupy the main hall, an offering box, incense burners, candles, fruit and flowers beneath their tranquil gaze. Behind are the halls of the patron Buddha, bodhisvatta, or patriarch of the temple, and further back, the abbots' living quarters and meditation rooms.

Aside from the Buddhist temples introduced in the bicycle tours, the following are worth a visit:

☐ **White Dagoba Temple (*Baitasi*)**: In the West City District, on the north side of Fuchengmennei Street. The towering white dagoba, looking much like the onion in Beihai Park, was designed by a Nepalese architect in the Yuan Dynasty. Reopened in 1980 after use as a factory in the Cultural Revolution, it's a good place to miss the crowds and enjoy the tinkling of bells that drive away evil spirits.

☐ **Big Bell Temple (*Dazhongsi*)**: In the Haidian District, on Second Ring Road. This Qing Dynasty temple (built in 1733) is best known for its forty-six ton bell (the largest in China, second largest in the world) inscribed with the entire text of the Lotus Sutra. Cast under Emperor Yongle's direction, it was moved here in 1743. The museum includes another some 160 bells of various sizes and tones.

☐ **Temple of the Origin of the Dharma (*Fayuansi*)**: In the Xuanwu District, north of Wanshou Park. This large complex, built in 696 in the Tang Dynasty, includes an impressive collection of rare Buddhist treasures. It also houses the **Beijing Buddhist Academy,** a training center which prepares young monks to enter monasteries around the country.

☐ **Temple of Universal Succour (*Guangjisi*)**: In the West City District, on Fuchengmennei Street. Built in the Jin Dynasty, renovated in the Ming, this temple is home to the Chinese Buddhist Association and usually only open to Buddhist groups and scholars. A smile at the gatekeeper on a quiet day may, however, be the right ticket in.

☐ **Yellow Temple (*Huangsi*)**: In the Andingmen area, beyond Second Ring Road. Built in the Qing Dynasty to welcome the fifth Dalai Lama to Beijing, this Tibetan Buddhist temple is officially open only to high-ranking Lamas, though some intrepid travelers have been known to make their way in. Its distinctive gold and white dagoba can be seen from a distance.

☐ **Temple of the Pool and Wild Mulberry (*Tanzhesi*)**: In the Mengtougou District on Tanzhe Mountain, two hours by bus from downtown. The oldest temple in Beijing, this complex was built along the contour of a hill in the Western Jin Dynasty. *Tan* refers to the pool above the temple, *zhe* to the wild mulberries that grow in abundance over the hills.

☐ **Temple of the Ordination Altar (*Jietaisi*)**: At the foot of Ma'anshan (Saddle Mountain) eight kilometers southeast of Tanzhesi. A Tang Dynasty relic from 622, this temple is known for its three-level stone terrace that was used to initiate monks and its ancient pines and cypresses.

Daoism

Even more than Buddhism, Daoism is hard pressed to be called a religion. It is a philosophy, a conceptual framework, a way of life. It is most purely Chinese, having been born in and reared on the Chinese experience.

Early Daoist thought was first described in a collection of writings called the *Daodejing* (credited to a man named Laozi who lived in the Spring and Autumn Period around 600 B.C.) and the book of the Master of the Southern Flowering Land (c. 500-300 B.C.). The central concept in this doctrine is *Dao*, the Way, the harmonious, spontaneous relationship of human beings to the great cosmos; the understanding of nature as the largest whole, the macrocosm, and human beings and other living creatures as the microcosm; the subsequent release into the whole, freeing oneself from the constraints of individuality.

Popular Daoist "religion," which developed later in the Han Dynasty, elaborated on these ideas and created a Daoist Heaven with a multitude of divinities. Their priests came to be known for magic and immortality; many believed they could fly through the air and walk through walls. Over time, Daoists gained a reputation for their association with secret societies and rebellious peasant groups.

There are only a couple Daoist temples left in Beijing. To an inexperienced eye, they appear scarcely different from their Buddhist counterparts. The lay-out is similar: major halls lined up south to north and divided into numerous courtyards. Many of the deities are the same. Decoration and symbolic motif do, however, vary widely. Daoist temples overflow with the life-prolonging *lingzhi* (long life mushroom), Daoist immortals, cranes, and the eight trigrams from the *Book of Changes*.

The largest and most important Daoist temple in Beijing is the **White Cloud Temple** (*Baiyunguan*) described in the *Spring* section. There's also the **Temple of the Taishan God** (*Dongyuemiao*) on Shenlu Street in the Chaoyang District. Built in the Yuan Dynasty to honor the God of Tai Mountain (one of the five Daoist holy mountains), it was at one time the largest Daoist temple in northern China.

Islam

Founded by the Prophet Mohammed, Islam is the religious faith of Muslims. Mohammed was born in A.D. 570 in Mecca (Saudia Arabia). His first revelation from God (Allah) in 610 and later visions were compiled into the Muslim holy book, the *Koran*. Arabian and Persian traders brought the religion, along with their wares, to China in the seventh century. They settled into their own communities in the west and southeast, converting pockets of Han Chinese along the way.

Today Islam is observed by ethnic minorities, particularly those of Turkic origin, and Chinese Muslims. Mosques are thicker in the west of China where these groups tend to live. There is a substantial community of Muslims in Beijing, mostly Hui and Uyghur people from Xinjiang who populate their own neighborhoods (Ox Street in the *Spring* section and Weigongcun in the *Summer* section).

In Chinese, mosques are called *qingzhensi* (temple of purity) or *libaisi* (temple of worship). They're usually rectangular, with a large open courtyard, a covered prayer hall, side rooms for ritual ablution (necessary before worship), and one or more minarets from which the muezzin calls the faithful to prayer. Women and men are strictly separated. Orientation to Mecca is of primary importance; a niche in the far end of the prayer hall marks the direction worshipers must face when kneeling in prayer to Allah.

Aside from the **Ox Street Mosque**, the **Dongsi Mosque** at the Dongsi intersection in the northeast part of town is an important center for Chinese and foreign Muslims. First built in 1447, its Chinese-style courtyards have been renovated more than once; now only the Prayer Hall dates back to the Ming. Headquarters to the Beijing branch of the Chinese Islamic Association, you must call first for a visit.

Christianity

Christianity has a long and rocky history in China. The Nestorians from Persia brought it with them in the seventh century when they entered by the silk road, the very same traveled by Islam and Judaism. Father John Montecorvino of Rome came 600 years later, followed by the Italian Jesuit Matteo Ricci, who taught science and technology in conjunction with his religion. In the nineteenth century Protestant and Roman Catholic missionaries rushed to the scene, not uncoincidentally, with the western drive for expansion.

Tensions and superstitions in the late 1800s incited the Chinese to rise in occasional outbursts against the well-meaning missionaries and their converts. The Boxer Rebellion of 1900 left 250 foreigners, mostly missionaries, and thousands of Chinese Christians dead. For the Western powers, it was the right excuse to slap around the Qing government and tighten their fist of control (as evidenced by the city-wide demolition campaign and the expansion and fortification of the foreign legation quarter).

Nowadays, Christian worship is restricted to official churches. The Chinese government has no relations with the Vatican, and only the Patriotic Catholic church is permitted to conduct services. The Protestants' activities are likewise unified under the Beijing branch of the Chinese Christian Council (the amalgamation of some sixty churches that were up until 1958 represented by foreign missions).

There are four major Catholic churches in Beijing:

☐ **South Church (*Nantang*)**: In the Xuanwu District, northeast of the Xuanwumen intersection. Beijing's oldest church, Nantang was founded in the late sixteenth century when Christianity was first getting a firm foot in the door with the Jesuit Fathers Matteo Ricci (1552-1610) and Adam Schall von Bell (1592-1666). The present building dates only to 1904, its predecessor having met the wrath of the Boxers in 1900.

☐ **West Church (*Xitang*)**: Near the Xizhimen Gate at the northwest corner of the Inner City. Like the others, Xitang has had a troubled past. Built in the 1700s, destroyed in 1811. Rebuilt in 1867, destroyed in 1900. Rebuilt in the early twentieth century.

☐ **North Church (*Beitang*)**: In the West City District, north of Xi'anmen Street. Built in 1887, it was besieged for seven weeks by the Boxers in 1900 before

Japanese troops rescued the 3,000 Christians and fifty allied soldiers holed up inside. Beitang was badly damaged in the Cultural Revolution and converted to a factory warehouse before it was reopened in 1985. Its gothic-style white facade makes it one of the best dressed churches in Beijing.

☐ **East Church (*Dongtang*)**: In the East City District, on the northern end of Wangfujing. Site of Adam Schall von Bell's house, Dongtang was founded in 1666, burned to the ground in 1900 and rebuilt soon thereafter. Primary school students now fill the grounds during the week but empty out for mass on Sundays.

Two Protestant churches in Beijing conduct Sunday services:

☐ **Rice Market Church (*Mishitang*)**: In the East City District, on North Dongdan Street. Named after the old market place, this small gray brick building with Chinese-style roofs is a domestic project; Chinese Christians put it up in 1915 completely independent of foreign missionaries. Home to the Beijing branch of the Chinese Christian Council, it's the center of official Protestant faith in China.

☐ **Crock and Tile Market Street Church (*Gangwashitang*)**: In the West City District, at 57 South Xisi Street. Built in the early twentieth century for the London Missionary Society, its large hall can pack in five hundred of the faithful. Like Mishitang, it gets its name from the local market.

What To Do

Entertainment

There's a whole world of amusing, enlightening activities beyond the bike lane in Beijing. The *China Daily*, an English-language newspaper distributed nationwide, carries a list of cultural events and shows. You can phone ahead to make reservations, go through CITS (China International Travel Service) or show up and take your chances. Ticket prices have never been very high, but in this new age of economic reform, everything is creeping upward. Evening performances are generally scheduled for 7:15 pm.

Around the turn of the century, teahouses, wine shops and opera were *the* night life in Beijing. Opera has been the only real survivor, though teahouses, like the ones described in the *Spring* section (Lao She Teahouse in Dazhalan and Tianqiao Fortune Tea Garden in the Tianqiao district), have been revived for tourists.

Dating from only 1790, when a provincial troupe came to perform for Emperor Qianlong, Beijing opera is a combination of singing, speaking, dancing, mime and acrobatics that can go on for up to six hours. You may not last through the closing scene, particularly if shrill tunes and crashing cymbals are not to your taste.

Nightly performances at the Liyuan Theater in the Qianmen Hotel on Yong'an Road (Tel. 301-6688) present a selection from the longer operas for the tourist crowd.

Acrobatics are another favorite. Performers of this art have awed and entertained for over two thousand years with their balancing and contorting. In Beijing, it's still one of the cheapest amusements going. For acrobatic shows, ballet, dance performances, theater and cinema, check the newspaper's daily listings.

As for music, international concert artists occasionally breeze through town, and the weekends are often host to underground rock'n'roll parties. Discos at the big joint-venture hotels (Holiday Inn Lido, China World Hotel, Kunlun, etc.) draw the dancing crowd. If you really get stuck with nothing to do, you can always join 80% of the local population and flip on the tube.

Shopping

Beijing is fast becoming a shopper's paradise—but at a price. Imported luxury items, unheard of a year ago, now line the shelves of many a classy emporium. Even alley shops have a whole new range of snacks to entice the neighborhood kids. Choice and quality are naturally reflected on the price tag. For domestic goods, it's still much cheaper than what you'd pay in the West for comparable products, but no longer does the outrageous Chinese bargain exist. Though prices in stores are generally fixed, the fine art of bargaining thrives in the stalls and open-air markets.

Gift shops around the city are loaded with Chinese arts and crafts—cloisonné, papercuts, jade carvings, silk kites, embroidered blouses, lacquer ware, crocheted tablecloths, jewelry, bamboo, batik, etc. You won't have to search if these are on your list, but remember that tourist hotels charge tourist prices. You'll save a bundle by paying a visit to the Arts and Crafts Service on Wangfujing or the White Peacock Arts and Crafts World on the northern Second Ring Road.

Some of the best bargains to be had in Beijing are on clothes, especially down coats, leather jackets and silk wear. Export quality fashion at comparatively low prices can be found in the outdoor markets on "Silk Alley" (Xiushui Street) east of the Friendship Store, on Yabao Road west of Ritan Park, and in the alleys directly south of the zoo.

If you're looking for antiques and used goods, there's the Chaoyang Antique Market on Yabao Road northwest of Ritan Park. Cultural Revolution alarm clocks (featuring a Red Guard waving the Little Red Book around the hour), cigarette calendars from the thirties and other curios can be found in the long line of stalls along the northern edge of the Temple of Heaven. The bird market around the Chegongzhuang subway station is another possibility. In all cases, the coveted object may be of questionable antiquity. Stiff bargaining is the rule. Another option is to buy from state stores where, though you pay for it, you can be sure you're getting the real thing.

The following are the major shopping districts in Beijing:

☐ **Wangfujing**, a north-south street east of the Beijing Hotel, described in the *Autumn* section. Home of the city's largest department store and numerous specialty shops, this historical uptown shopping district is soon to enter the modern era with a classy joint-venture mall. Fast food restaurants and foreign shops have already taken up some of the prime real estate.

☐ **Qianmen**, the area south of Tian'anmen Square, described in the *Spring* section. Aside from shops along Qianmen Street, selling everything from minority musical instruments to peddle sewing machines, there's the jumble of *hutongs* around Dazhalan. Here you will find some of the oldest stores and retired theaters in the capital. Liulichang, the restored antique and book center of imperial times, can be reached through the *hutongs* to the west.

☐ **Xidan and Dongdan**, parallel north-south streets several blocks each from the Forbidden City. Xidan, on the west side, is described in the *Autumn* section. Fast food restaurants and shiny new shops carrying imported goods are, like everywhere in Beijing, claiming a stake in these old commercial districts.

Where To Eat

Everybody knows about Peking roast duck. But what about Mongolian hot-pot? Muslim BBQ? Kentucky Fried Chicken? Northerners love their meat, their oil, their salt—dinner without several kinds and cuts of meat is hardly considered a meal. Unlike steak and large slab meat eaters, the Chinese chop theirs into bite-sized pieces, fry in oil or braise over coals and serve up ready to be chopsticked. Vegetarians, however, must not despair. Fresh vegetables are aplenty, everything from the ubiquitous *youcai* (bokchoy) to a variety of fungal growth. Tofu abounds.

A skilled Chinese cook takes the right ingredients, dices-slices-or-chops, adds the right seasonings and fries-boils-or-steams for the right length of time under the right temperature. Though to the inexperienced, Chinese food seems a single species, regional variation in seasoning and cooking style has distinguished four main types:

Shandong Cuisine: Also known as northern cuisine, this style originated in the Yellow River valley. Dishes are characterized by light, mellow flavors.

Sichuan Cuisine: From the upper reaches of the Changjiang (Yangtze) River, dishes are hot and spicy.

Jiangsu Cuisine: Popular in the middle and lower reaches of the Changjiang River and southeastern coastal areas, the food is generally stewed, braised, boiled or simmered in its own juice. Sweetness prevails.

Guangdong (Cantonese) Cuisine: From the Pearl River valley and southern coastal areas, dishes are stir-fried, deep-fried, braised or stewed. Seafood abounds, though almost anything that walks or jumps is fair game.

The number of eating establishments in the capital seems to increase daily. Imported joint-venture hotels bulge with international jet-set menus—Italian, Mexican, Indian, Mediterranean, Korean, etc. Fast food chains, mostly of American heritage, raise aspirations and flashing neon to the skyline. Small privately owned shops line the alleys, frying up wholesome home-style food to feed the masses. There is a dish for every taste in Beijing, a dinner for every pocketbook.

The following list of places to eat is by no means complete. Many hotel restaurants are not included, nor the burgeoning family of western fast food. Most are established restaurants with reasonable hygienic standards and menus in English. As any seasoned traveler knows, successful dining in unfamiliar territory is best accomplished by keeping your nose to the ground and an ear raised to recommendation. The adventurous will find in back lanes and side alleyways a wealth of small shops eager to oblige the hungry tourist. Courage and a finger for pointing (to vegetables in the back or dishes served on the table) are all that are needed to communicate your wishes to the chef.

One last word: Lunch usually runs from 11 am to 12 pm, dinner from 5 pm to 7 pm. Pulling in much later than 8 pm in the winter is a good way to ensure you go to bed hungry that night; summer hours extend late into the evening.

Beijing Cuisine (Peking Roast Duck)

Qianmen Quanjude (The Old Duck)
32 Qianmen Street
Tel. 511-2418

Wangfujing Duck Restaurant (The Sick Duck—so named for its proximity to the Capital Hospital)
13 Shuaifuyuan Lane; one block north of the Beijing Hotel
Tel. 55-3310

Hepingmen Quanjude (The Big Duck)
14 West Qianmen; just south of the Hepingmen intersection
Tel. 301-8833

Mongolian Hot-Pot/Muslim Food

Donglaishun
16 Jinyu Lane; north of the Dongfeng Market on Wangfujing.
Tel. 55-2092

Hongbinlou
82 West Chang'an Avenue; just east of the Xidan intersection. Tel. 601-4832

Kaorouji (Grille restaurant)
14 East Qianhai; on the northeastern side of Qianhai Lake. Tel. 44-5921

Kaorouwan
93 Fuxingmennei Avenue
Tel. 601-3123

Imperial Cuisine

Fangshan Restaurant
Beihai Park; on the Jade Islet
Tel. 401-1879

Li Jia Cai (Li Family Restaurant)
11 Yangfang Hutong, Denai Street
Tel. 601-1915

Tingliguan (Listening to the Orioles Pavilion)
Summer Palace (Yiheyuan)
Tel. 258-1608, 258-1955

Shandong Cuisine

Confucian Heritage Restaurant
3 West Liulichang, Xuanwu District
Tel. 33-0689

Cuihualou Restaurant
60 Wangfujing; fifteen minute walk north of Beijing Hotel. Tel. 55-4581

Fengzeyuan (Horn of Plenty)
Xingfu Sancun, Chaoyang District
Tel. 421-7508

Ritan Gongyuan (Temple of the Sun) Restaurant
Ritan Park; northeast corner, through the north entrance.
Tel. 59-2648

Tongheju
3 South Xisi Street; near the Xisi intersection on North Xidan Street.
Tel. 602-0925

Sichuan Cuisine

Emei Restaurant
North Yuetan Street; next to Yuetan (Temple of the Moon) Park at the intersection of Lishi Road and North Yuetan Street.
Tel. 511-2014

Shenxian Douhua Zhuang
Ritan Park; southwest gate.
Tel. 500-5939

Sichuan Restaurant
51 West Rongxian Hutong; south of the Xidan intersection.
Tel. 603-3291

Jiangsu Cuisine

Laozhengxing Restaurant
46 Qianmen Street
Tel. 511-2145

Guangdong (Cantonese) Cuisine

Dasanyuan Restaurant
50 West Jingshan Street
Tel. 44-5378, 401-3920

Jing Cheng Restaurant
A-27 Baishiqiao Road, Haidian District
Tel. 89-8626, 802-2288

Meishicheng (Hong Kong Food City)
18 Donganmen Street
Tel. 513-6668

Pearl Seafood Restaurant
111 East Dianmen Street
Tel. 512-3294

Renren (Beijing-Hong Kong joint venture)
18 East Qianmen Street
Tel. 511-2042, 511-3408

Vegetarian/Health Food

Gongdelin Vegetarian Restaurant
(Yangzhou-style)
158 South Qianmen Street
Tel. 75-0867

Zhen Shuzhai Restaurant
74 Xuanwumennei; north of the Xuanwumen intersection.
Tel. 65-3181

International Cuisine Asian And Western

Check the joint-venture hotels for their restaurant listings. The following are independent businesses:

Baiyun Restaurant (Japanese)
Youhao Guest house, 7 Houyuan'ensi, Jiaodaokou.
Tel. 44-1036 (ext. 264)

Chalon Restaurant (Japanese)
50 East Tiantan Road
Tel. 701-2660

Beijing Doosan Restaurant (Korean)
Hualong Street, Nan Heyan
Tel. 512-9130, 512-9135

Shan Fu Restaurant (Korean)
West Deshengmen Street, Huitong Ci
Tel. 601-4569

Liyuan Restaurant (Thai)
8 West Huangchenggen
Tel. 601-5234

Moscow Restaurant (Russian)

Beijing Exhibition Center, Xizhimenwai Street; between the zoo and the exhibition center.
Tel. 89-4454

Snacks

Duyichu (Steamed Dumplings)
36 Qianmen Street
Tel. 511-2093, 511-2094

Longfusi Snackbar (*Ludagun*: Sweet steamed rolls)
106 Longfusi Street Tel. 44-2062

Goubuli Baozi (Stuffed steamed buns)
155 Di'anmenwai Street
Tel. 44-2460

Night Markets set up outside in the evening sell fried, steamed, boiled, and braised snacks. Hours generally run from 5 pm to 9 pm. Below are a few that cater to night-time snackers:

Donganmen Street; between the east gate of the Forbidden City and Wangfujing.

East Chang'an Avenue; east of the Beijing Hotel, near McDonald's.

Fuxingmenwai Street; in front of the Yanjing Hotel.

Xizhimenwai Street; across from the Capital Gymnasium, west of the Xiyuan Hotel.

Zhongguancun; Haidian Road, south of Beijing University.

Where To Stay

Finding the right place to hole up in Beijing is no longer a struggle. Hotels, like restaurants, come in a range of prices for a range of tastes. They are rated with stars, from one to five. Below is a partial list, with details on budget hotels for budget travelers. <B> indicates bicycle rental service.

Budget
(Dormitory Accommodations) ★

Beijing University Guesthouse/Shaoyuan Lou: <B> About 45 minutes from downtown on the Beida campus. Double rooms and shared bath; meals available in the foreign students' dining hall. Beijing University, Zhongguancun, Haidian District. Tel. 255-2471 (ext. 3365)

Other universities in town that offer relatively inexpensive lodging:

Beijing Language Institute (*Yuyan Xueyuan*)

Beijing Teachers' University (*Beishida*)

Central Academy of Fin Arts (*Meishu Xueyuan*)

People's University (*Renmin Daxue*)

Qinghua University (*Qinghua Daxue*)

Feixia Hotel: <B> 4 km west of Tian'anmen (ten minutes on #48 bus which stops at the Beijing Railway Station and Tian'anmen Square). Dorm-style standard rooms with no bath and three beds; "first class" rooms with two beds and bath. All have air-conditioning and TV.
Building Number 5, Xili Xibianmen,
Xuanwu District
Tel. 301-2228

Jingtai Hotel: <B> To the south of the city on a small *hutong* off Anlelin Road (the first stop after the canal on #39 bus from the railway station), this hotel has become an increasingly popular choice with budget travelers in recent years.
65 Yongwai Jingtaixi, Fengtai District
Tel. 76-4675

Qiaoyuan Hotel: <B> 6 km south of Tian'anmen near Yongdingmen Railway Station; last stop on the #20 bus line. Young budget travelers from all over the world gather here to enjoy the cheap 20-bed dormitories.
Dongbin He Road, Yongdingmen, Fengtai District
Tel. 303-8861

Tiantan Sports Hotel: <B> Near the northeast corner of the Temple of Heaven (about 4 km from Tian'anmen), this hotel was built for sports

delegations but has been taken over by backpackers in recent years. From Chongwenmen, take bus #39, 41 or 43.
10 Tiyuguan Road, Chongwen District
Tel. 701-3388

Economy ★★

Beiwei Hotel <B>
13 Xijing Road, Xuanwu District
Tel. 301-2266

Hademen Hotel <B>
2 Chongwenmenwai Street, Chongwen District
Tel. 701-2244

Huabei Hotel <B>
3 Huangsi Street, East City District
Tel. 202-2266

Ritan Hotel
1 Ritan Road, Chaoyang District
Tel. 512-5588

Shangyuan Hotel <B; guests only>
4 Zixiansi, Xizhimenwai, Haidian District
Tel. 831-1122

Middle Of The Road ★★★

Dongfang Hotel <B>
11 Wanming Road, Xuanwu District
Tel. 301-4466

Minzu Hotel <B>
51 Fuxingmennei Street, West City District
Tel. 601-4466

Qianmen Hotel <B>
175 Yongan Road, Xuanwu District
Tel. 301-6688

Tianqiao (Rainbow) Hotel <B>
11 Xijing Road, Xuanwu District
Tel. 301-2266

Xinqiao Hotel <B>
2 East Jiaominxiang, Chongwenmen, Chongwen District
Tel. 513-3366

Xiyuan Hotel <B>
5 Erligou, Haidian District
Tel. 831-3388

First-Class ★★★★

Jinglun (Beijing-Toronto) Hotel <B>
3 Jianguomenwai Street, Chaoyang District
Tel. 500-2266

Friendship Hotel
3 Baishiqiao Road, Haidian District
Tel. 849-8888

Holiday Inn Lido <B>
Capital Airport Road, Jiangtai Road, Chaoyang District
Tel. 500-6688

Jianguo Hotel <B>
5 Jianguomenwai Street, Chaoyang District
Tel. 500-2233

Mandarin (Xindadu) Hotel <B>
21 Chegongzhuang Street, West City District
Tel. 831-9988

Peace Hotel <B>
3 Jinyu Hutong, Wangfujing, East City District
Tel. 512-8833

Deluxe *****

Beijing Hotel <B>
33 East Changan Avenue, East City District
Tel. 513-7766

China World Hotel <B; free for guests>
1 Jianguomenwai Street, Chaoyang District
Tel. 505-2266

Diaoyutai State Guesthouse
Sanlihe Road, Haidian District
Tel. 803-1188

Great Wall Sheraton <B>
North Dongsanhuan Road, Chaoyang District
Tel. 500-5566

Kunlun Hotel <B>
South Xinyuan Road, Chaoyang District
Tel. 500-3388

Palace Hotel <B; guests only>
8 Jinyu Hutong, Wangfujing, East City District
Tel. 512-8899

Shangri-La Hotel
29 Zizhuyuan Road, Haidian District
Tel. 841-2211

Traveler Basics

Visas

Visas for individual travel can be readily obtained at Chinese embassies and consulates abroad and at travel agencies in Hong Kong. A group visa may be issued to groups of ten or more.

Tourist visas are generally valid for two months from the date of issue for a single visit of 30 to 60 days. Validity extends *not* from the date of entry, but from the date of issue—so don't get your visa too far in advance of your trip. You may extend your visa for up to a month at the Foreign Affairs Section of the local Public Security Bureau. In Beijing, go to:

Municipal Public Security Bureau, Visa Dept
 85 Beichizi Street. Tel. 55-3102
 Hours: 8:30-11:30 am, 1-5 pm Mon. to Fri.;
 8:30-11:30 am Saturday; closed Sun.

Applications at the embassies require two passport-size photos and a nominal fee for paper-work processing. Travel agencies in Hong Kong offer a wide variety of options, charging higher rates for faster service. For more information, ask at the Chinese embassy or consulate near you:

Australia
247 Federal Highway, Watson, Canberra,
2600 ACT

Canada
411-415 Andrews Street, Ottawa, Ontario
KIN 5H3

New Zealand
2-6 Glenmore Street, Kelburr, Wellington

United Kingdom
31 Portland Place, London WIN 3AG

United States
2300 Connecticut Avenue NW,
Washington, DC 20008

Consulates in the US:
1450 Laguna Street, San Francisco, CA 94115
520 12th Avenue, New York, NY 10036
104 S Michigan Avenue, Suite 1200, Chicago, 60603
3417 Montrose Blvd, Houston, Texas 77006

When in China, keep your passport with you wherever you go. You will need it to check into your hotel, to change travelers' checks at the bank and to purchase airline and train tickets. Chinese law requires foreigners to carry passports at all times. The police don't make a habit of checking, but you never know when you might need it.

What to Bring

Almost everything these days is available in the capital. No longer do you have to cart in your deodorant and batteries, coffee and tampons. Many stores around town, large and small, carry a wide range of bourgeois western products to meet the needs of today's modern populace. So don't panic if you forget your sunblock or shampoo. But be prepared to fork out several times the amount you'd pay back home for the same brand.

In the clothing department little is lacking. Though large people may have difficulty finding their size, Beijing is a wonderful place to stock up on fashion. The only absolute must-brings are a comfortable pair of walking shoes (or boots in the winter) and wool socks (again, for the winter). Other winter necessities—silk long johns, down coats, leather gloves—are available in season.

Shorts and T-shirts are just right for summer days; add a light layer in the evening or when it rains. For spring and autumn, layers are the key. Evenings are considerably cooler than daytime—a sweater and jacket, preferably of the wind-breaking type, are in order.

You should also bring a good pair of sunglasses and a water bottle for bike treks. First-aid and sewing kits, alarm clocks and pocket knives always come in handy. Don't forget your pump, tools and spare parts if you're going to bring your own bike.

Money

At the time of writing, there are still two forms of currency in China, *Renminbi* (RMB— people's money) and Foreign Exchange Certificates (FEC—tourist money, issued for use by foreigners and compatriots from abroad). Though officially they are of equal value, FEC is still worth slightly more than RMB on the black market. The rage over FEC a couple years back has cooled considerably with the government's recent devaluation program, and street money changers have turned their interest to the more reliable US Dollar. FEC will eventually be phased out altogether.

The exchange rates for FEC as of fall 1993 are approximately:

```
A$1    =  4.00 yuan
C$1    =  4.60 yuan
HK$1   =  0.70 yuan
Y1000  = 48.00 yuan
UK 1   =  8.30 yuan
US$1   =  5.80 yuan
```

When you change your foreign currency at the bank, you will be given FEC. In general, you will be required to use FEC in all the tourist hotels and restaurants, at sightseeing spots, for train and airline tickets and for international communications. Private businesses—restaurants and clothing stalls, even the larger stores—as well as taxis and buses can not demand FEC, but many of them may try to get away with it and then give you change in RMB.

The basic unit of each currency is the *yuan* (known as *kuai* in spoken Chinese). It is divided into 10 *jiao* (called *mao*); the *jiao* is divided into 10 *fen* (pronounced "fun"). In other words, there are 100 portions of fun in 1 *yuan*.

FEC, identifiable by the English on the back, comes only in paper notes. They are the 1, 5, 10, 50 and

100 *yuan*; and the 1 and 5 *jiao* (or 10 and 50 *fen*). Change for anything smaller is given in RMB.

RMB comes in both paper notes and coins. Paper notes are issued for the *yuan*: in denominations of 1, 2, 5, 10, 50 and 100, for the *jiao*: in denominations of 1, 2 and 5, and for the *fen*: in denominations of 1, 2 and 5. Coins now exist for the 1 *yuan*, the 1 and 5 *jiao*, and the 1, 2 and 5 *fen* denominations.

Foreign currency and internationally recognized travelers' checks can be changed at the Bank of China, in tourist hotels and in some of the larger stores. Keep your vouchers when you change your money; you will need these to reconvert your FEC back to foreign currency when you leave the country. In fact, according to regulation, you will need vouchers equal to at least double the amount you want to reconvert, meaning you spent half of what you originally changed—a governmental ploy to ensure spending. RMB is not supposed to be taken out of the country and can not be reconverted to foreign currency.

Credit cards are now widely used in Beijing as well as other major cities in China. American Express, Visa, MasterCard, Diner's Club, Federal Card, JCB and China's own—the Great Wall Card—are honored at most tourist hotels, restaurants and stores.

Health

Few foreign tourists get sick in Beijing. Those who do probably conducted themselves as if they were back home, ignoring the basic rules of hygiene in a country which uses human night soil as fertilizer:

- Do not drink unboiled water.

- Do not eat uncooked food in places with questionable sanitation.
- Peel your fruit.
- Wash your hands before eating.

Throat colds (upper respiratory infections) are a common ailment in dry, dusty Beijing. Make sure you drink lots of water and eat plenty of oranges and pears. If something stronger hits, the following hospitals are used to dealing with foreigners:

Peking Union Medical College Hospital (or Capital Hospital)
Xiehe Yiyuan
North Dongdan Street
Tel. 512-7733

Sino-Japanese Friendship Hospital
Zhong Ri Youhao Yiyuan
North Hepingli Street
Tel. 422-1122

Sino-German Policlinic (with 24 hour ambulance service)
Zhong De Zhensuo
Basement, Landmark Tower, 8 East Sanhuan Road; Tel. 501-1983, 501-6688 ext. 20903

Beijing Friendship Hospital
Youyi Yiyuan
Yong'an Road, Tianqiao
Tel. 301-4411

Transportation Around Town

Aside from your trusty two-wheeler, what other forms of transportation are there in Beijing? Buses, trolley buses, the subway, minibuses and taxis. Buses (with red stripes) and trolley buses (with blue stripes) criss-cross the city in a web of convenience. The subway makes a circle, following the route of Second Ring Road (*Erhuan Lu*), and shoots off to the west at Fuxingmen station. All the above are notoriously crowded during the day, but cheap (a couple *mao*) and a good way to mash elbows with the people. Keep an eye on your personal belongings.

Minibuses run fixed routes during the day along transit lines. For example, of the fleet that leaves from Beijing Railway Station, there are minibuses up to the Summer Palace (passing through Qianmen or Xidan) and to Yongdingmen Station in the south. These should cost only several *yuan*, but the ticket takers are not exactly girl scouts when they see the chance for extra income.

Taxis, of course, are the most convenient, clean, costly form of transportation. You can find them waiting in front of big hotels or hail one from the curb. Regular taxis charge a couple *yuan* per kilometer with a start-up fee of around 12 *yuan*. A better deal are the "small loafs" (*xiaomianbao*), pint-size vans that race around the city for 1 *yuan* per kilometer. The 90 *yuan* trip to the airport can be cut to around 50 *yuan* in a *xiaomianbao*.

Transportation Out of Town

Your departure from Beijing should be planned well in advance. Of the three options—long distance bus, train and plane—the bus requires the least amount of preparation. On some routes you can just buy your ticket and go.

Long distance bus stations to outlying areas are located on the perimeter of the city: at Dongzhimen (north-east), Guangqumen (south-east) and Tianqiao (on the west side of the Temple of Heaven). Buses to Tianjin leave regularly from the front of Beijing Railway Station.

For train tickets, go to the "International Passenger Booking Office" at the Beijing Railway Station (Tel. 512-8931, 512-9515). It's open daily, 5:30-7:30 am, 8-11:30 am, 1-5:30 pm and 7:30 pm-12:30 am. Tickets can be booked five days in advance for locations all over the country. Go early if you want a sleeper.

Beijing is connected by a great aerial web to the rest of the world. Thirty-nine international routes serve twenty-five countries, including three or four direct flights to Hong Kong a day. Air China (formerly known as CAAC) and its various subsidiaries cover all major domestic locations and many minor ones as well.

Most major hotels have an Air China reservation desk. Or go directly to the source:

Air China, Head Office
15 West Chang'an Avenue
Tel. Domestic flight reservations: 601-3336
    International flight reservations: 601-6667
    Ticket office information: 601-7755
    Capital Airport information: 456-3604

The following international airlines also have offices in Beijing:

Aeroflot
Hotel Beijing-Toronto
Tel. 500-2412

Air France
China World Trade Center
Tel. 505-1818

All Nippon Airways
China World Trade Center
Tel. 505-3311

British Airways
SCITE Tower
Tel. 512-4070

Canadian Airlines
Jianguo Hotel
Tel. 500-1956

Dragonair Hong Kong
China World Trade Center
Tel. 505-4343

Ethiopian Airlines
China World Trade Center
Tel. 505-0314

Finnair
SCITE Tower
Tel. 512-7180

Iran Air
International Building
Tel. 510-4040

Japan Airlines
Hotel New Otani
Tel. 513-0888

JAT Yugoslav Airlines
Kunlun Hotel
Tel. 500-3388 ext. 426

LOT Polish Airlines
Jianguo Hotel
Tel. 500-2233

Lufthansa
SCITE Tower
Tel. 512-3636

Malaysia Airlines
China World Trade Center
Tel. 505-2681

Northwest Airlines
Jianguo Hotel
Tel. 500-4529

Pakistan International
China World Trade Center
Tel. 505-2256

Philippine Airlines
China World Trade Center
Tel. 505-0136

Qantas
Hotel Beijing-Toronto
Tel. 500-2481

Romanian Airlines
Romanian Embassy, Ritan Road, East 2 Street
Tel. 532-3552

SAS-Scandinavian Airlines
SCITE Tower
Tel. 512-0575

Singapore Airlines
China World Trade Center
Tel. 505-2233

Swissair
SCITE Tower
Tel. 512-3555

Thai International
SCITE Tower
Tel. 512-3881

United Airlines
SCITE Tower
Tel. 512-8888

☐ **Capital Airport** (Tel. 55-5402, 55-2515, 55-7396) is located 29 kilometers north-east of the city. Air China buses make the 50-minute shuttle between the airport and the Air China Building at Xidan for 8 *yuan* apiece. Though they claim to leave every twenty minutes, it's more likely that they'll go whenever they fill up. A taxi or the local bus No 359 to Dongzhimen are your alternatives.

Information and Phone Numbers

Extracting accurate information from the Chinese can be a laborious process. Not always, but often, it becomes an exercise in fortitude and second-guessing. There is both the history of secretiveness when dealing with foreigners and the Socialist regard of information as capital, to be bestowed upon those in favor. From a cultural standpoint, there is the problem of "face" (some refer to this as "status"). In order to save face for both parties, people will at times make up an answer rather than admit ignorance. They may also tell you whatever it is they think you want to hear—regardless of the question.

Obtaining accurate information in the tourist hotels or at CITS (China International Travel Service) should present no problem, but be wary of direction-givers on the street. Remember the three-times rule: Ask three times. Even then you may get three different answers.

Though phone numbers change periodically in Beijing, the following list should be of some help:

Tourist hotline (24 hour service)	513-0828
Emergency Center	120
International Operator	115
Domestic Operator	113
Municipal Directory Information	114
Domestic Directory Information	116
Weather	117
Time	121
CITS	515-8566
Public Security, Visa Department	55-3102

Public Security, Foreigners' Section	512-8871
Bank of China	33-8521
Capital Airport	55-5402
	55-2515
	55-7396
Beijing Railway Station	512-8931
	512-9515
Capital Taxi Company	86-3661
Beijing Taxi Company	832-2561
Embassies: Australia	532-2331
Canada	532-3536
France	532-1331
Germany	532-2161
Italy	532-2131
Japan	532-2361
New Zealand	532-2731
UK	532-1961
USA	532-3831

Bicycle Rental

How to enjoy the pleasures and hassles of biking in Beijing, or anywhere in China for that matter? One option is to pack up your lightweight touring cycle and bring it along. Some do and claim it's the only way to see the country. Though definitely a superior choice for comfort and reliability, an obvious drawback is security.

Bicycle theft, especially in the cities and especially of expensive, top-quality models, is a fact of life in China. Most urban shopping and entertainment areas have guarded daytime parking lots with special double-rate sections for "good" bikes, but the norm is to secure the freestanding bike with an internal lock or loose chain, a tenuous situation at best. Not only that, but the old ladies and gentlemen who watch these lots go home at night, chaining together the bicycles left after closing time for next day pick-up. A stationary bike hitching post is naturally preferable but not always available.

Another consideration is bike parts. An imported bicycle needs imported parts, which you will supply, because the local repair shops will not. That goes for the tire pump as well. Bring your own.

The second option for the would-be bicyclist is to rent. Not always comfortable, not always reliable, but guaranteed to multiply your adventure-possibility quotient many times. A rental bike is like a horse for hire—over-used, under-appreciated and often poorly maintained. A few newer ones are out there but always get snatched up before the kickstand's down. Most of the nicer hotels offer a good quality selection, but if you rent from the shops or schools, you can expect to ride away with the standard heavy-duty one-speed Chinese model, easy enough for Beijing's flat terrain, safe enough for public parking.

Rental bikes return to the ranch in dubious condition, and Chinese bikes in particular are known for their brake ailments. A stop-on-a-dime braking system is hard to come by, but you should at least be able to pull up short without wearing your shoes down. Tires are also important but often neglected. Besides a firm pump-up, you need a good tread to help with the braking and swerving. Make sure none of the moving parts are about to fall off or the stationary parts moving. Ride your intended around to get a feel for the seat. It can be raised or lowered, and if all else but your rear end is satisfied, a couple *yuan* will pad it with a velour seat cover from one of the department stores.

A large cash deposit or a piece of I.D. like your passport is required as security. In smaller towns, a driver's license, student card or other such dubious forms of identification have been known to work, but don't expect big-city folk to be so easily fooled.

Schools and Shops

The following schools and shops in Beijing provide rental bikes at cut-rate prices (Y3 to Y10 a day). The schools are inconveniently located at the far northwest edge of town, but if you're staying out there anyway or plan to rent for several days, it may be worth it. Avoid the lunch time (11:30 am to 1:30 pm) siesta.

Beijing Language Institute
15 Xueyuan Road, Haidian District; at the western gate.

Beijing University
Zhongguancun, Haidian District; at the foreign students' dormitory and outside the Building for General Affairs.

Che-san Bicycle Repair Shop
Baishiqiao Road, Haidian District; northeast of the Beijing Library.

Chongwenmen Bicycle Repair Shop
94 Chongwenmen Street

Jianguomenwai Bicycle Repair Shop
Jianguomenwai Avenue; across the street from the Friendship Store.

Qinghua University
Qinghuayuan, Haidian District

Hotels

Most hotels also provide bike rental service (look for the <B> in the hotel list). Prices range from Y3 FEC a day to an outlandish Y72 FEC, calculated at Y3 an hour. In terms of both cost and quality, little relation appears to exist between a hotel's star count and its bicycle fleet. Big, expensive hotels generally do ask more, but small, cheaper hotels do not always ask less.

Bicycle Rental

Besides that, rental bikes are a mixed lot; you don't always get what you pay for, and sometimes you get much more.

The following is a list of the more reasonably priced hotel bike rental services:

Y3-Y10 per day
Qiaoyuan Hotel
Hademen Hotel
Feixia Hotel

Y20-Y25 per day
Beijing Hotel
Beiwei Hotel
Jinglun (Beijing-Toronto) Hotel
Kunlun Hotel
Tianqiao (Rainbow) Hotel
Tiantan Sports Hotel
Xiyuan Hotel

Bicycle Tours

The prospect of running loose through the streets of Beijing, map in hand, nose to the wind, eye to the sun, ducking in and out of *hutongs*, converging at whim with bike lane traffic, peering around the bend for who-knows-what-may-come-next, may strike some as an adventure fit for Indiana Jones. Guided bike tours are a good choice for those set on particular sights or interested in meeting a local guide. The following travel service centers organize group bike tours and provide bikes for rent:

China International Travel Service (CITS)
28 Jianguomenwai Street   Tel. 515-8566

Beijing China Travel Service
2 Chongwenmen Street
Tel. 701-3265

Huayuan International Travel Service
West Deshengmen Street
Tel. 601-4841

Survival Chinese

Beijing, closed for centuries to the outside world, is becoming increasingly accessible to those who can't speak Chinese. Staff in all the large hotels and tourist centers speak a reasonable level of English; even taxi cab drivers and shop assistants can pull out a few useful phrases. There will be times, however, when you'll have to rely on your own awkward pronunciation and bold ingenuity to get in or out of a situation. The following list should help some but there is no substitute for a traveler's phrase book (such as *Essential Chinese for Travelers* by Fan Zhilong).

Hello/How do you do	Ni hao	你好
Goodbye	Zai jian	再见
Thank you	Xie xie	谢谢
You're welcome	Bu ke qi	不客气
I'm sorry	Dui bu qi	对不起
That's alright/Never mind	Mei guanxi	没关系
I don't understand	Wo bu dong	我不懂
I can't speak Chinese	Wo bu hui shuo Hanyu	我不会说汉语
Can you speak English?	Ni hui shuo Yingyu ma?	你会说英语吗？
Where's the _____?	_____ zai nar?	在哪儿？
I'm lost	Wo mi lule	我迷路了
Please show me on the map	Qing zai ditu shang zhi gei wo kan	请在地图上指给我看
How far is it?	Duo yuan?	多远？
How much does it cost?	Duo shao qian?	多少钱？
That's too expensive	Tai guile	太贵了
I want to rent a bike	Wo yao zu yiliang zixingche	我要租一辆自行车
Do you have a newer model?	You meiyou geng xinde?	有没有更新的？
The brakes don't work	Shache huaile	刹车坏了
What's the rental fee?	Zu che duoshao qian?	租车多少钱？
How much for one day?	Duoshao qian yi tian?	多少钱一天？
How much for one hour?	Duoshao qian yi xiaoshi?	多少钱一小时？
How much is the deposit?	Yajin duoshao qian?	押金多少钱？
Please repair my bike	Qing xiuli wode che	请修理我的车
I have a flat tire	Wode chetai lou qile	我的车胎漏气了
Please raise the seat	Qing ba zuowei shenggao	请把座位升高
Please lower the seat	Qing ba zuowei fangxia	请把座位放下

English	Pinyin	Chinese
I	Wo	我
You	Ni	你
She/He/It	Ta	他, 她, 它
Hotel	Fan dian; Lu guan	饭店；旅馆
Hospital	Yi yuan	医院
Park	Gong yuan	公园
Store	Shang dian	商店
Post office	You ju	邮局
Road	Lu	路
Toilet	Ce suo	厕所
Restaurant	Fan guan	饭馆
Menu	Cai dan	菜单
Chopsticks	Kuaizi	筷子
Fork	Chazi	叉子
Spoon	Shaozi	勺子
Rice	Mi fan	米饭
Noodles	Mian tiao	面条
Bread	Mian bao	面包
Pork	Zhu rou	猪肉
Beef	Niu rou	牛肉
Chicken	Ji rou	鸡肉
Vegetables	Shu cai	蔬菜
Beer	Pi jiu	啤酒
Boiled water	Kai shui	开水
Bus stop	Gonggong qiche zhan	公共汽车站
Train station	Huoche zhan	火车站
Airport	Ji chang	机场
Taxi	Chuzu qiche	出租汽车
Telephone	Dian hua	电话
North	Bei	北
South	Nan	南
East	Dong	东
West	Xi	西
Left	Zuo	左
Right	You	右
Straight	Yi zhi	一直
Turn	Guai wan	拐弯

Today	Jin tian	今天
Tomorrow	Ming tian	明天
Day after tomorrow	Hou tian	後天
Yesterday	Zuo tian	昨天
Morning	Shang wu	上午
Noon	Zhong wu	中午
Afternoon	Xia wu	下午
Night	Wan shang	晚上
Day	Tian	天
Week	Libai	礼拜
Month	Yue	月
One	Yi	一
Two	Er	二
Three	San	三
Four	Si	四
Five	Wu	五
Six	Liu	六
Seven	Qi	七
Eight	Ba	八
Nine	Jiu	九
Ten	Shi	十
Hundred	Bai	百
Thousand	Qian	千
Ten thousand	Wan	万

Glossary

Bixi: A mythological animal resembling a tortoise reputed to have the strength to support tremendous weight. *Bixi* sculpted from stone are found in temples, gardens and cemeteries with heavy stone stelae on their backs.

Dian: In ancient times, a general term for large, tall buildings. It was later used in the names of halls where gods or Buddhas were worshipped, or where the emperor held audience and handled state affairs.

Hai: Sea or large lake, e.g., *Qianhai* (Front Lake).

Huabiao: An ornamental column, usually carved from stone, that was placed before palaces, city walls, bridges and tombs in ancient times. Coiling dragons or other designs decorate the stem, a sculptured cloud extends horizontally through the center near the top, and a stone beast squats in the dish above that. Two pairs to the north and south of Tian'anmen Gate are good examples.

Hutong: A lane or small alley. The word derives from Mongolian and means a passageway between tents or yurts.

Jie: Street; *Dajie* means avenue or boulevard, e.g., *Chang'an Dajie* (Chang'an Avenue or Chang'an Boulevard).

Joint-venture: A business jointly owned and managed by a group on the Chinese side and a foreign company.

Lou: A building of two or more stories, e.g., *Gulou* (Drum Tower).

Lu: Road, e.g., *Erhuan Lu* (Second Ring Road).

Men: A gate or door, e.g., *Tian'anmen* (Gate of Heavenly Peace).

Shi: Market, e.g., *Luomashi Dajie* (Mule and Horse Market Street).

Si: A Buddhist temple or monastery.

Stele: An ancient upright slab or pillar that was usually inscribed or sculptured and often used as a headstone.

Ta: Pagoda or stupa. *Ta* is the shortened form of what in ancient times was called *fota* (Buddha pagoda) or *baota* (precious pagoda). Most *ta* are either square or octagonal and were once used to store sutra scrolls or Buddhist relics.

Tan: Altar, e.g., *Tiantan* (Altar to Heaven, known commonly as Temple of Heaven).

Yuan: 1. A park or place for amusement, e.g., *Yiheyuan*, *Daguanyuan*; 2. An orchard, flower or vegetable garden.

Index

Acrobatic Rehearsal Hall, 105
Altar of Heaven, 108
American Embassy, 41
Ancient Observatory, 35, 37
Angler's Terrace, 13
Arrow Tower, 27
Arts and Crafts Exhibition Hall, 16
Arts and Crafts Service, 45, 162
Back Lake, 71
Beihai Park, 68, 77, 152, 167
Beijing, 149
Beijing Art Museum, 120
Beijing Department Store, 45
Beijing Library, 119, 115, 196
Beijing Railway Station, 34, 42, 175, 186, 187
Beijing University, 119, 137, 173, 180, 196
Beijing Zoo, 117
Bell Tower, 65, 66, 67
Bicycle Rental, 194
Big Bell Temple, 67, 152
Book City, 140
Botanical Gardens, 130
Bridge of Heaven, 106
Bridge of Vermilion Steps, 109
Bronze Pavilion, 126
Caishikou, 94
Capital Gymnasium, 117, 119, 173
Capital Library, 62
Central and South Lakes, 22, 78
Chairman Mao Memorial Hall, 24, 26

Index 209

Chang'an Market, 15
Changhe River, 120
Charlie's Ice Cream, 21
Che-san ("Bike-three") Bicycle Repair, 118, 119, 196
Chegongzhuang, 55, 51, 162, 178
Cherry Vale Garden, 131
China Airlines, 21
China Bookstore, 98
China International Travel Service, 13, 16, 166, 191, 197
Chinese-Japanese Friendship Association, 63
Chinese-Japanese Friendship Guesthouse, 63
Churches, 150
Circular Wall, 77
Commercial Press Bookstore, 96
Confucian Temple, 58
Dazhalan Market, 101
Di'anmen Street, 68, 79, 172
Diamond Throne Pagoda, 131
Ditan Park, 54
Dong'anmen Night Market, 47
Donglaishun, 46, 167
Drum Tower, 63, 64, 65, 68, 205
Duyichu, 100, 172
East Gate, 54
East Wind Market, 46
Echo Stones, 109
Echo Wall, 109
Eight Great Temples, 131
Entertainment, 160
Fangshan, 79, 167
Five Dragons Pavilion, 79
Five Pagoda Temple, 117
Food, 164
Forbidden City, 3, 8, 17, 144
Foreign Languages Bookstore, 46
Foreign Languages Bureau, 46
Fragrant Hills Park, 130
Friendship Hotel, 8, 119, 115, 136, 141, 177
Friendship Store, 38, 39, 141, 162, 196
Front Lake, 71, 210
Garden of Harmonious Virtue, 127
Gate Facing the Sun, 27

Gate of Exalted Civilization, 94
Gate of Moral Victory, 54
Gate of Proclaimed Military Prowess, 94
Glazed Tile Factory, 95
Gongdelin, 110
Grand Hotel de Pekin, 32
Grand View Garden, 88, 89
Great Hall of the People, 24, 25
Great Wall, 147
Haidian, 140, 141, 152, 170, 180, 176, 177, 178, 179, 196
Hall of Abstinence, 108
Hall of Benevolent Causation, 78
Hall of Benevolent Longevity, 127
Hall of Eternal Divine Protection, 57
Hall of Five Hundred Arhats, 131
Hall of Heavenly Kings, 79
Hall of Jade Ripples, 128
Hall of Joyful Longevity, 128
Hall of Limitless Pleasure, 129
Hall of Mathematics, 58
Hall of Medicine, 58
Hall of Perfection, 60
Hall of Pleasing Rue, 128
Hall of Prayer for Good Harvests, 109, 110
Hall of the Wheel of the Law, 57
Heavenly Kings, 57, 79
Hill of Long Life, 128
History Museum, 27, 29
Hortensia Isle, 77, 78
Hotels, 175
House of Leisure, 129
Imperial Academy, 59, 62
Imperial Palace, 148
Imperial Vault of Heaven, 108
Iron Screen, 79
Jade Lake Park, 12, 13
Jade Spring Mountain, 118, 130
Kunming Lake, 125, 127
Lamasery of Harmony and Peace, 55
Lao She Teahouse, 102, 166
Legation Quarter, 29, 30, 32
Liubiju, 102

Index 211

Long Corridor, 128, 129
Longevity Hill, 127, 128, 131
Lotus Flower Market, 76
Marble Boat, 126, 129
Military Museum, 15, 150
Minorities Cultural Palace, 16, 17, 149
Minorities Hotel, 16
Monument to the People's Heroes, 26
Moon Observation Tower, 92
Mosques, 150
Mount Miaofeng, 131
Municipal Indoor Ice Skating Rink, 117
Museum, 148
National Art Gallery, 48, 149
Neiliansheng Shoe Store, 104
Nest of Pines and Clouds, 129
New China Bookstore, 45
New Palace Gate, 125
Nine Dragon Screen, 79
Northern Lakes Area, 2, 55, 68, 73
Number Two Hospital for Infectious Diseases, 89
Olympic Hotel, 117
Ox Street, 91
Pagoda of Many Treasures, 132
Pagoda of Supreme Height, 130
Palace of Peace and Harmony, 56, 57
Park of Good Health and Harmony, 125
Park of Perfection and Brightness, 133
Pavilion for Inspecting Old Script, 78
Pavilion of Ten Thousand Happinesses, 57
Peking Union Medical College Hospital, 42, 185
People's Bank of China, 16, 184, 192
People's University, 140, 175
Prince Gong's Mansion, 74
Prospect Hill, 48, 77, 79, 80
Purple Bamboo Park, 120
Qianhai, 67, 71, 74, 76, 81, 167, 210
Qianmen, 27, 29, 45, 88, 94, 163, 186
Qinghua University, 137, 175, 196
Quanjude Peking Roast Duck Restaurant, 101, 166
Revolving Scripture Repository, 129
Ritan Park Restaurant, 40

Riufuxiang, 102
Rongbaozhai, 97
Seventeen Arch Bridge, 127
Shangri-La Hotel, 121, 179
Shenxian Douhua Zhuang, 40, 169
Silver Ingot Bridge, 71
Soong Ching Ling, 72
South Church, 95, 157
South Lake Island, 22, 127
St. Michael's Catholic Church, 32
Strolling Through Painting Hall, 129
Summer Palace, 4, 22, 29, 119, 120, 123, 125, 126, 127, 129, 131, 133, 168, 186
Suzhou Street, 131, 132
Telegraph Office, 21
Temples, 150
Temple of Azure Clouds, 130
Temple of Heaven, 2, 8, 40, 54, 88, 84, 105, 106, 107, 162, 175, 187, 205
Temple of Heavenly Peace, 87
Temple of Longevity, 120
Temple of the Reclining Buddha, 130
Temple of the Sun Park, 40
Three Flavors, 17
Tian'anmen Gate, 24, 25, 28, 210
Tian'anmen Square, 7, 22, 145, 148, 163, 175
Tianfu Douhua Zhuang, 20
Tianqiao, 150
Tianqiao Department Store, 106
Tianqiao Fortune Teahouse, 106, 166
Tongrentang Traditional Medicine Shop, 103
Tower of Buddhist Fragrance, 129
Tower of Orderly Administration, 65
Tower of Realizing Shamefulness, 65
Wangfujing, 2, 17, 32, 33, 44, 45, 47, 95, 101, 149, 158, 162, 167, 168, 172, 178, 179
Weigongcun, 142, 155
West Access Gate, 84
West Gate, 52
West Heavenly Gate, 107
West Lake, 73
Western Hills, 71, 118, 125, 129

White Cloud Japanese Restaurant, 63
White Cloud Temple, 85, 155
White Dagoba, 78
White Peacock Art World, 54, 162
Working People's Cultural Palace, 28
Xidan Market, 19
Xiushui Street, 41, 162
Yandai Lane, 68
Yanjing Hotel, 15, 172
Youth Activity Center, 52
Zhongnanhai Compound, 22
Zhongshan Park, 28

ESSENTIAL RESOURCES for Your Trip to China

To help you prepare for your trip to China, here are the essential ingredients of a traveler's handbag:

TOURIST ATLAS OF CHINA
Handy small maps of over 56 cities and major attractions with diagrams of museums and parks. Valuable for planning itineraries, and easy to carry along because of its compact size. Cartographic, 1988, 99 pp., paper. #TOATCH...........................$9.95

FULL-COLOR POLITICAL MAP
with place names in *pinyin*. (42" x 30"). #1034-6..$5.95

MAP OF BEIJING
Useful city map includes diagrams of parks and museums, and a list of important addresses and telephone numbers to hotels, restaurants, museums, and transportation offices. 1982. 28" x 20". #0980-1..$2.95

SILK BROCADE JOURNAL
Keep a record of your travels. (5" x 8"). #D500SB...$5.95

ESSENTIAL CHINESE FOR TRAVELERS
by Fan Zhilong

". . . handy reference . . . this is also a practical guide for the tourist."
—BOOKLIST

A must for tourists, business people and scholars traveling in China, this pocket-sized phrasebook has over 2,000 useful words and phrases. Easy to use, it's divided into convenient subject categories: transportation, money, food, business, shopping, etc. It uses up-to-date colloquial Chinese as spoken in the PRC today. CBP, 1988. 160 pp. #ESCHTR......book......$6.95 ■ #ESCHBT......book & 90 min. tape.....$14.95

SIGHTS WITH STORIES IN OLD BEIJING
Edited by Chinese Literature

The ancient sites of Beijing all seem to have a legend associated with them. Here is a collection of local folklore about the Great Wall, Forbidden City, Lama Temple and other sites. For travelers, armchair and otherwise. Panda, 1990. 189 pp. #2087-2................$5.95

✔ CHINA BOOKS' TRAVELER'S CHECKLIST
Can't remember everything to take with you? We have prepared a simple checklist to help insure you don't forget the most important things—and it's free! Just write to us and ask for it. We will include it in your order, or send it to you (please send self-addressed stamped envelope).

Call or write for our free catalog of books and other items from and about China — we have something for everyone!

CHINA BOOKS & PERIODICALS, INC.
2929 Twenty-fourth Street, San Francisco, CA 94110
415-282-2994 ❖ FAX: 415-282-0994